# FREE VIDEO     FREE VIDEO

### *Essential Test Tips* Video from Trivium Test Prep!

Dear Customer,

Thank you for purchasing from Trivium Test Prep! We're honored to help you prepare for your police exam.

To show our appreciation, we're offering a **FREE *Essential Test Tips* Video by Trivium Test Prep**.* Our video includes 35 test preparation strategies that will make you successful on your police exam. All we ask is that you email us your feedback and describe your experience with our product. Amazing, awful, or just so-so: we want to hear what you have to say!

To receive your **FREE *Essential Test Tips* Video**, please email us at 5star@triviumtestprep.com. Include "Free 5 Star" in the subject line and the following information in your email:

1. The title of the product you purchased.
2. Your rating from 1 – 5 (with 5 being the best).
3. Your feedback about the product, including how our materials helped you meet your goals and ways in which we can improve our products.
4. Your full name and shipping address so we can send your **FREE *Essential Test Tips* Video**.

If you have any questions or concerns please feel free to contact us directly at: 5star@triviumtestprep.com.

Thank you!

– Trivium Test Prep Team

*To get access to the free video please email us at 5star@triviumtestprep.com, and please follow the instructions above.

# Police Officer Exam Study Guide 2025-2026:

Full Practice Test, Chapter Review Questions, Detailed Answer Explanations, and Prep Book

[6th Edition]

B. Hettinger

Copyright © 2025 by Trivium Test Prep

ISBN-13: 9781637985311

ALL RIGHTS RESERVED. By purchase of this book, you have been licensed one copy for personal use only. No part of this work may be reproduced, redistributed, or used in any form or by any means without prior written permission of the publisher and copyright owner. Trivium Test Prep; Accepted, Inc.; Cirrus Test Prep; and Ascencia Test Prep are all imprints of Trivium Test Prep, LLC.

Trivium Test Prep is not affiliated with or endorsed by any testing organization and does not own or claim ownership of any trademarks. All test names (and their acronyms) are trademarks of their respective owners. This study guide is for general information and does not claim endorsement by any third party.

Image(s) used under license from Shutterstock.com

# TABLE OF CONTENTS

**INTRODUCTION** ................................. i

## 1 READING COMPREHENSION    1
Introduction ......................................... 1
Topic and Main Idea ........................ 3
Supporting Details ............................ 5
Drawing Conclusions ....................... 6
The Author's Purpose and
Point of View ..................................... 7
Comparing Passages ......................... 9
Meaning of Words .......................... 10

## 2 WRITING    15
Introduction ..................................... 15
The Parts of Speech ....................... 16
Punctuation ..................................... 18
Phrases .............................................. 19
Clauses .............................................. 19
Common Grammatical Errors ..... 20
Vocabulary ....................................... 26
Spelling ............................................. 31

## 3 MATHEMATICS    39
Mathematical Operations .............. 39
Operations with Positive and
Negative Numbers .......................... 40

Fractions ........................................... 40
Decimals ........................................... 42
Ratios ................................................ 43
Proportions ...................................... 43
Percentages ...................................... 43
Estimation and Rounding ............. 44
Units ................................................. 44
Perimeter and Area ........................ 45

## 4 REASONING FOR LAW ENFORCEMENT    49
What is Reasoning? ........................ 49
Inductive Reasoning ....................... 49
Deductive Reasoning ..................... 52
Problem Sensitivity ........................ 54
Spatial Orientation ........................ 56
Information Ordering .................... 57
Memorization .................................. 58
Visualization .................................... 59
Selective Attention ......................... 59
Flexibility of Closure ..................... 60

## 5 PRACTICE TEST    63
Answer Key ................................... 121

# Online Resources

Trivium Test Prep includes online resources with the purchase of this study guide to help you fully prepare for your Police Officer exam.

### Review Questions
Need more practice? Our review questions use a variety of formats to help you memorize key terms and concepts.

### Flash Cards
Trivium Test Prep's flash cards allow you to review important terms easily on your computer or smartphone.

### Cheat Sheets
Review the core skills you need to master the exam with easy-to-read Cheat Sheets.

### From Stress to Success
Watch "From Stress to Success," a brief but insightful YouTube video that offers the tips, tricks, and secrets experts use to score higher on the exam.

### Feedback
Let us know what you think!

Access these materials at:

**www.triviumtestprep.com/police-officer-online-resources**

# INTRODUCTION

Congratulations on choosing to take the next step in your career in law enforcement by preparing for your local or departmental police exam! By purchasing this book, you've taken an important step on your path to becoming a law enforcement or corrections officer.

This guide will provide you with a detailed overview of the content covered on most national police and corrections exams, so you know exactly what to expect on exam day. We'll take you through all the important concepts and give you the opportunity to test your knowledge with practice questions. Even if it's been a while since you last took a major exam, don't worry; we'll make sure you're more than ready!

## What is the Police Exam?

Police and highway patrol academies, police departments, and departments of corrections across the United States use comprehensive exams to assess candidates. For example, the state of California Commission on Peace Officer Standards and Training (POST) has developed the PELLETB (the POST Entry-Level Law Enforcement Test Battery). In Florida, most police academies and Florida Highway Patrol require the CJBAT (Criminal Justice Basic Abilities Test). Several agencies throughout the nation, including Chicago, Philadelphia, Pittsburgh, and state police in Missouri, Arkansas, Maine, Pennsylvania and elsewhere use the NCJOSI (National Criminal Justice Officer Selection Inventory). Michigan uses the MCOLES (Michigan Commission on Law Enforcement Standards). Check with your agency or academy to determine which exam you need to prepare for. Many community colleges also offer police exams.

## What's on the Police Exams?

Different exams test different subjects. Still, there are a few major topics covered on almost every exam. Candidates are evaluated on their reading, language, and reasoning skills. Some exams also test basic math and quantitative reasoning skills. Most tests have around one hundred multiple-choice questions and are approximately two hours long. The number of questions and exact time vary by test.

## Reading Comprehension Questions

**READING COMPREHENSION** questions test your ability to understand written texts, analyze the information presented, and draw conclusions from it. You will be asked to identify the main idea, details, and/or draw conclusions from reading passages. You may also be asked about vocabulary. You do not need to use outside information for these questions.

## Writing Questions

**WRITING** questions test your grammatical and writing skills. You may be asked about subject-verb agreement, spelling, or sentence structure. Some questions ask you to complete a sentence by choosing the correct word; other questions ask you to choose the clearer of two sentences.

Many exams test spelling skills. You might be asked to identify a misspelled word in a sentence or complete a sentence by choosing the correctly spelled word in a multiple-choice question.

## Reasoning Questions

There are several types of reasoning questions on the major police exams. This book provides an in-depth discussion of reasoning as well as several reasoning practice question sets.

**INDUCTIVE REASONING** questions ask you to draw conclusions from quantitative information provided in the form of charts or graphs. Questions might concern the impact of policies or certain trends over time. Applying your inductive reasoning skills using the information provided in the visual aids will allow you to answer the questions.

For **DEDUCTIVE REASONING** questions, you will be provided with a written textual excerpt from state law or a typical precinct policy. Then, you will be presented with a situation related to that written material and asked a question about it. To find the correct answer, you will need to use the legal information provided to resolve the situation. The appropriate application of general rules to a specific situation is *deductive reasoning*.

**INFORMATION ORDERING** questions ask you to place a series of statements into chronological or logical order. You will be presented with five or six disordered statements, and then you will choose the answer that places them in the correct order.

**PROBLEM SENSITIVITY** questions test your ability to understand if a situation is deteriorating or if something is likely to go wrong. In these questions, you will read a description of a situation and determine what the issue is and how to resolve it.

**SPATIAL ORIENTATION** questions determine your ability to understand where you are located in relation to something else. On the exam, you will review maps to determine the fastest routes between locations or where a vehicle or suspect has traveled. Similarly, **VISUALIZATION** questions ask you to determine how a pattern of shapes fits together.

**SELECTIVE ATTENTION** and **FLEXIBILITY OF CLOSURE** questions test your attention to detail. You must identify certain patterns or correctly choose how many times a number, letter, or symbol appears in an image or text.

**MEMORIZATION** questions test your observation skills. You will have two minutes to review a photograph or picture, and then you will be asked questions about details in the image.

Not every police exam contains each kind of reasoning question, but this book provides practice for all of them.

## ADMINISTRATION AND TEST DAY

Different police exams like the PELLETB, CJBAT, NCJOSI, and more, are administered by participating law enforcement agencies and academies. To register for an exam, you must directly contact the participating agency or academy where you are applying. You may take most exams in a pencil-and-paper format or a computer-administered format. Check with your agency to be sure.

On test day, arrive early. Check with the facility or participating agency to make sure you know what type of identification to bring (usually government-issued photo identification). Bring at least two sharpened No. 2 pencils. Personal belongings, cell phones, and other electronic, photographic, recording, or listening devices are not permitted in the testing center. Many testing centers offer lockers to secure your personal items, but you should check beforehand with the facility to be sure storage is available.

## TIPS FOR TACKLING MULTIPLE-CHOICE QUESTIONS

The following tips assume you have a basic understanding of test taking: how to follow test proctor instructions, properly record answers, make sure the answer for the right question is recorded, and review an answer sheet before submitting it. If you do nothing else to prepare, learn these quick tips—they will help you focus your efforts and use your time wisely.

### Handling Distractors

*Distractors* are the incorrect answer choices in a multiple-choice question. They "distract" you from the correct answer. Read and answer the question below:

> **Criminals are people who violate _____.**
> A) Penal Code 62
> B) civil procedure
> C) martial law
> D) criminal laws

The correct answer choice is D, *criminal laws*. The other, incorrect answer choices—the distractors—are designed to distract the inattentive test taker by "sounding" right or formal. While choices A and C may be partially correct—breaking a specific penal code (criminal) or martial (civilian-imposed military) law may be a crime—neither is the *best* answer choice.

Be sure to read the question for context and tone, and try to determine what is being asked. The preceding question asks for a general definition and uses wording from the question as part of the correct answer. While a criminal might violate a *specific* penal code or martial law, generally, violations can be of *any* criminal law. Because criminals are guilty of crimes and *all* criminal laws involve or pertain to crime, choice D is the *best* answer.

### Develop a Time Strategy

Most police exams are around two hours long. Pay attention to the time: note the start and end time for each section prior to beginning, and make a goal to complete each question in one minute or less. One minute seems like a short amount of time, but it actually is not. You will likely complete most questions in less than thirty seconds. Develop your strategy such that you finish the easier questions quickly, allowing more time to focus on the difficult questions.

Don't spend too much time on difficult questions; instead, mark them, skip them, and come back when you have time.

### Focus on the Question

Read the question carefully. Words sometimes change meaning based on context. Context is the part of a communication that comes before or after a specific word or passage and provides clarity or meaning. Make sure you read and understand the question before selecting an answer. Read the following sentences:

> The police **arrested** Chad when he was eighteen years old.
>
> Chad is thirty-two years old, but his emotional development was **arrested** when he was eighteen years old.

The word *arrested* is used correctly in both sentences, but it has different meanings depending on the context.

Try to think of an answer before looking at the choices. This can keep you from being distracted by the incorrect answer choices and help you more easily identify the answer.

### Correct is Not Always Best

Several answers could be *correct*, or close to correct, but you must choose the *best* answer choice. Beware of answer choices that are close to the correct answer but are merely distractions.

### Use the Process of Elimination

Eliminate answer choices you know are incorrect; choose your answer from the remaining choices.

For "all of the above" and "none of the above" answer choices, look for options that include elements that break the "all" or "none" rule, such as a true element in a group of false elements or vice versa. If one element does not belong with the rest of the group's elements, then the answer cannot be *all*, or *none*, of the above.

Reread the question and remaining answers and select an answer choice.

## ABOUT THIS GUIDE

This guide will help you master the most important test topics and develop critical test-taking skills. We have built features into our books to prepare you for your tests and increase your score. Along with a detailed summary of the test's format, content, and scoring, we offer an in-depth overview of the content knowledge required to pass the test. Throughout the guide, you'll find sidebars that provide interesting information, highlight key concepts, and review content so that you can solidify your understanding. You can also test your knowledge with sample questions throughout the text as well as practice questions. We're pleased you've chosen Trivium to be a part of your journey!

# READING COMPREHENSION

## INTRODUCTION

In the land of movies and television, law enforcement officers are rarely shown reading. Dirty Harry, John McClane, Horatio Caine, or Andy Sipowicz would be hard-pressed to pick up the penal code, case notes, or even a newspaper! But in the real world, where shooting up the entire downtown area; costing the city and county millions of dollars in repair costs and civil suits; and turning your back on suspects to don sunglasses can get you fired, sued, or hurt, reading is a huge part of the job.

Law enforcement officers spend a considerable amount of time reading reports, case law, statutes, subpoenas, warrants, investigative notes, memos and policy changes, news reports about policing and the community, and more. Understanding what you read is paramount because it may dictate how you do the job.

> You do not need to use outside knowledge on reading comprehension questions. Remember, the answer is located within the passage.

Misunderstanding what you read could cost you your job. Reading comprehension is one of the most important aspects of law enforcement. Police officer exams test applicants' reading comprehension abilities by presenting a passage to read, then asking several questions about the passage's content. The following information provides tips and tricks to improve your skills and navigate the reading comprehension section of the exam.

### Reading for Understanding

Reading for understanding is different from reading for entertainment. Rather than simply skimming a passage for generalized information, the reader must dig more deeply into the text, make inferences and connections, and evaluate and interpret ideas and information. However, an integral part of reading comprehension is answering questions about the information. To be proficient at comprehension, readers must master several tasks while reading a particular passage:

**DIFFERENTIATE FACT FROM OPINION.** Many readers cannot tell the difference between fact and opinion. Contrary to popular belief, fact and opinion are not opposites; instead, they are differing types of statements. A FACT is a statement that can be proven by direct or objective evidence. Juries are called the "finders of fact" because they use the evidence presented to prove a statement. On the other hand, an OPINION, though it may be based in fact, is a statement established using belief or judgment and cannot be objectively proven true or false. Opinions are not necessarily wrong; they simply are not fact.

> Law enforcement officers often summarize in conversations. To ensure understanding, officers may repeat, in their own words, information a victim or suspect provides. The victim or suspect generally confirms or adjusts the restated information. To practice summarizing, after reading, take the information that is most important and restate it in your own words.

**DISTINGUISH BETWEEN WHAT IS IMPORTANT AND WHAT IS SIMPLY INTERESTING.** When determining what is important in a passage, think about the main point and tone. What is the author trying to say? What is the main point? Information that tends to strengthen or weaken the main point is important. Information that does not strengthen or weaken the main point is simply interesting.

**DETERMINE CAUSE-AND-EFFECT RELATIONSHIPS.** Determine if there is a cause-and-effect relationship between pieces of information contained in the passage. Determining cause-and-effect relationships is important in comprehension as well as in establishing potential outcomes.

Look for words that show causal relationships, such as *because, since, therefore, thus,* and *so.*

**COMPARE AND CONTRAST IDEAS AND INFORMATION.** Connecting words often indicate transition within a passage. Understanding transitions can help keep you on track with the author's main point, rather than confusing you with opposing points of view in the passage. Look for words that show a shift in the author's position, such as *however, but, rather, in contrast,* and *although.*

**DRAW CONCLUSIONS.** Law enforcement officers regularly make inferences, draw conclusions, and make determinations based on information presented. After reading the passage, ask yourself:

- What judgments can be made based on the information provided?
- What evidence included in the passage supports that judgment?
- Are there other interpretations that can be made using the provided information and evidence?

## Question Types

Reading comprehension tests generally use seven basic question types. They are explored in more detail in the chapter.

1. **WHAT'S THE MAIN POINT?** These questions ask you to identify the author's thesis or hypothesis. A question stem relating to this question type might ask, "The passage was primarily concerned with which of the following?" Check the thesis statement or conclusion for the answer to these types of questions.

2. **WHAT'S THE SUPPORTING IDEA?** These questions generally ask you to locate specific information. A question stem relating to this question type might ask, "The passage mentions each of the following EXCEPT…" You may need to reread the passage to find the answer. You might look for keywords in the answer choices to help steer you in the right direction.

3. **DRAWING INFERENCES.** Questions that require you to draw inferences often ask, "The passage implies which of the following?" The answer choices generally will closely imitate the text of the passage and rely upon specific facts provided.

Read the passage carefully. Do not skim the passage. Read it two or three times to ensure you understand what the passage is communicating. Remember, this section is examining comprehension. Reading too quickly can cause you to miss important information.

4. **WHAT'S THE TONE?** These questions ask you to identify the author's attitude. Question stems generally ask, "The author's tone is best described as …"

5. **APPLY THE THEME TO OTHER CIRCUMSTANCES.** Questions requiring you to apply information from the passage to a similar situation often take the following form: "The author would most likely agree with which of the following?" There is no shortcut or trick to answering these question types. The key is identifying the heart of the passage and relating it to similar answer choices.

6. **LOGICAL REASONING.** This question style is the reverse of the "Application" question style. Logical reasoning questions ask you to take information from *outside* the passage and apply it to the passage to make determinations. An example of a logical reasoning question might be "Which of the following, if true, would most weaken the main point of the second paragraph?" Understanding the author's main point or argument and using your reasoning abilities to determine the value of answer choices will help you answer these questions.

> Read the passage before the question. Reading the question first can distract you from the main point of the passage. An error is more likely if you answer the question prematurely and without full understanding.

7. **RELATING DIFFERENT IDEAS.** These questions require you to determine the relationship between different ideas or parts of the passage. Questions are framed in a variety of ways, but they might ask how two paragraphs relate to each other or how an idea in one sentence contrasts with an idea later in the passage.

## TOPIC AND MAIN IDEA

The **TOPIC** is a word or short phrase that explains what a passage is about. The **MAIN IDEA** is a complete sentence that explains what the author is trying to say about the topic. Generally, the **TOPIC SENTENCE** is the first (or near the first) sentence in a paragraph. It is a general statement that introduces the topic so the reader knows what to expect.

The **SUMMARY SENTENCE**, on the other hand, frequently (but not always!) comes at the end of a paragraph or passage because it

> To find the main idea, identify the topic and then ask, *What is the author trying to tell me about the topic?*

wraps up all the ideas presented. This sentence summarizes what an author has said about the topic. Some passages, particularly short ones, will not include a summary sentence.

Table 1.1. Identifying Topic and Main Idea

Noise complaints are one of the most common calls received by police officers in cities and suburban areas. Close quarters and strong personalities make it more likely that neighbors will butt heads; the officer's job is to keep the peace. Usually, an officer can solve the problem by warning the offender. Most people will immediately turn down their music or end a late-night party when they find out they risk a hefty fine. On rare occasions, officers will issue citations for violating city ordinances or will arrest offenders for crimes like disorderly conduct.

| | |
|---|---|
| **TOPIC SENTENCE** | Noise complaints are one of the most common calls received by police officers in cities and suburban areas. |
| **TOPIC** | noise complaints |
| **SUMMARY SENTENCE** | Close quarters and strong personalities make it more likely that neighbors will butt heads; the officer's job is to keep the peace. |
| **MAIN IDEA** | Officers respond to noise complaints, which are very common in crowded areas, to restore order. |

### Examples

1. **Topic**

    Police dogs usually work from six to nine years. K-9 officers have a variety of professional responsibilities: sniffing out explosives and narcotics, finding missing persons and human remains, and protecting officers. Many of them retire to live a comfortable life with their handlers, who know them better than anyone.

    What is the topic of the passage?

    **(A)** dog lifespan

    **(B)** police dogs

    **(C)** dog handlers

    **(D)** canine retirement

2. **Main Idea**

    The Battle of the Little Bighorn, commonly called Custer's Last Stand, was a battle between the Seventh Cavalry Regiment of the US Army and the combined forces of the Lakota, the Northern Cheyenne, and the Arapaho tribes. Led by war leaders Crazy Horse and Chief Gall and religious leader Sitting Bull, the allied tribes of the Plains Indians decisively defeated their US foes. Two hundred and sixty-eight US soldiers were killed, including Lieutenant Colonel George Armstrong Custer, two of his brothers, his nephew, his brother-in-law, and six Indian scouts.

    What is the main idea of this passage?

    **(A)** Most of Custer's family died in the Battle of the Little Bighorn.

    **(B)** The Seventh Cavalry Regiment was formed to fight Native American tribes.

    **(C)** Sitting Bull and George Custer were fierce enemies.

    **(D)** The Battle of the Little Bighorn was a significant victory for the Plains Indians.

# Supporting Details

Statements that describe or explain the main idea are **supporting details**. Supporting details are often found after the topic sentence. They support the main idea through examples, descriptions, and explanations.

Authors may add details to support their argument or claim. **Facts** are details that point to truths, while **opinions** are based on personal beliefs or judgments. To differentiate between fact and opinion, look for statements that express feelings, attitudes, or beliefs that cannot be proven (opinions) and statements that can be proven (facts).

To find supporting details, look for sentences that connect to the main idea and tell more about it.

Table 1.2. Supporting Details and Fact and Opinion

Police academies have strict physical requirements for cadets. Cadets must pass fitness tests and train daily. As a result, some new recruits worry about their physical fitness before heading into the academy. Some graduates suggest focusing on core strength. Others believe that boxing is the best workout. We feel that cardiovascular activity is the most important exercise.

| | |
|---|---|
| **SUPPORTING DETAILS** | Cadets must pass fitness tests and train daily. |
| **FACT** | Police academies have strict physical requirements for cadets. |
| **OPINION** | We feel that cardiovascular activity is the most important exercise. |

### Examples

3. **Supporting Details**

   Increasingly, companies are turning to subcontracting services rather than hiring full-time employees. This provides companies with advantages like greater flexibility, reduced legal responsibility to employees, and lower possibility of unionization within the company. However, this has led to increasing confusion and uncertainty over the legal definition of employment. Courts have grappled with questions about the hiring company's responsibility in maintaining fair labor practices. Companies argue that they delegate that authority to subcontractors, while unions and other worker advocate groups argue that companies still have a legal obligation to the workers who contribute to their business.

   Which detail BEST supports the idea that contracting employees is beneficial to companies?

   **(A)** Uncertainty over the legal definition of employment increases.
   **(B)** Companies still have a legal obligation to contractors.
   **(C)** There is a lower possibility of unionization within the company.
   **(D)** Contractors, not companies, control fair labor practices.

4. **Fact and Opinion**

   An officer cited a motorist for reckless driving. The driver was performing unsafe maneuvers. The motorist was "doing donuts," rotating the vehicle. The officer observed this activity in a parking lot after dark. The officer wrote a citation. In addition, the vehicle was impounded.

   Which statement from the passage is an opinion?

**READING COMPREHENSION**

**(A)** An officer cited a motorist for reckless driving.

**(B)** The driver was performing unsafe maneuvers.

**(C)** The motorist was "doing donuts," rotating the vehicle.

**(D)** In addition, the vehicle was impounded.

## Drawing Conclusions

| Look for facts, character actions and dialogue, how each sentence connects to the topic, and the author's reasoning for an argument when drawing conclusions. |
|---|

Readers can use information that is **EXPLICIT**, or clearly stated, along with information that is **IMPLICIT**, or indirect, to make inferences and **DRAW CONCLUSIONS**. Readers can determine meaning from what is implied by using details, context clues, and prior knowledge. When answering questions, consider what is known from personal experiences and make note of all information the author has provided before drawing a conclusion.

Table 1.3. Drawing Conclusions

When the Spanish-American War broke out in 1898, the US Army was small and understaffed. President William McKinley called for 1,250 volunteers to serve in the First US Volunteer Cavalry. The ranks were quickly filled by cowboys, gold prospectors, hunters, gamblers, Native Americans, veterans, police officers, and college students looking for an adventure. The officer corps was composed of veterans of previous wars. With more volunteers than it could accept, the army set high standards: all the recruits had to be skilled on horseback and with guns. Consequently, they became known as the Rough Riders.

| QUESTION | Why are the volunteers named Rough Riders? |
|---|---|
| EXPLICIT INFORMATION | Different people volunteered, men were looking for adventure, recruits had to be extremely skilled on horseback and with guns due to a glut of volunteers. |
| IMPLICIT INFORMATION | Men had previous occupations; officer corps veterans worked with volunteers. |
| CONCLUSION DRAWN | The men were called Rough Riders because they were inexperienced yet enthusiastic to help with the war and were willing to put in extra effort to join. |

### Example

**5. Drawing Conclusions**

"Swatting" is a dangerous practice. Someone falsely reports a crime in progress at a location to attract a large number of police to the site. The false crime usually involves hostages or a similar violent scenario, so police are prepared for confrontation. In fact, the term swatting is derived from the name for those police who specialize in such situations: the SWAT team, which carries high-caliber weapons and deploys flash bangs and tear gas. In a swatting incident, innocent citizens are shocked by a sudden police raid on their home. Likewise, police ready to face a violent perpetrator are surprised to find a family eating dinner or watching TV. The confusion caused by the false information and urgency of the raid make it very dangerous for all involved. Tragic outcomes are not uncommon.

Which conclusion about the effects of swatting is most likely true?

(A) Swatting is increasingly common, thanks to social media.
(B) Swatting mostly occurs where there are large SWAT teams.
(C) Swatting is usually harmless, though a waste of police time.
(D) Swatting can result in injury or death to innocent citizens or officers.

# The Author's Purpose and Point of View

The **author's purpose** is his or her reason for writing a text. Authors may write to share an experience, to entertain, to persuade, or to inform readers. This can be done through persuasive, expository, and narrative writing.

**Persuasive writing** influences the actions and thoughts of readers. Authors state an opinion, then provide reasons that support the opinion. **Expository writing** outlines and explains steps in a process. Authors focus on a sequence of events. **Narrative writing** tells a story. Authors include a setting, plot, characters, problem, and solution in the text.

> Use the acronym P.I.E.S.—*persuade, inform, entertain, state*—to help you remember elements of an author's purpose.

Authors also share their **point of view** (perspectives, attitudes, and beliefs) with readers. Identify the author's point of view by word choice, details, descriptions, and characters' actions. The author's attitude, or **tone**, can be found in word choice that conveys feelings or stance on a topic.

**Text structure** is the way the author organizes a text. A text can be organized to show problem and solution, comparison and contrast, or even cause and effect. Structure of a text can give insight into an author's purpose and point of view. If a text is organized to pose an argument or advertise a product, it can be considered persuasive. The author's point of view will be revealed in how thoughts and opinions are expressed in the text.

Table 1.4. The Author's Purpose and Point of View

Officer ride-alongs are a great way for community members to get to know law enforcement officers. They are a valuable opportunity for students, journalists, community leaders, and those considering a career in law enforcement to learn more about the day-to-day experiences of police business. In a ride-along, you join an officer as he or she responds to calls, stops cars, and interacts with the public. Riders can ask questions and see the world from the perspective of a cop. Ride-alongs are a wonderful way for members of the public to learn about policing.

| | |
|---|---|
| **AUTHOR'S PURPOSE** | persuade readers of the benefit of ride-alongs |
| **POINT OF VIEW** | advocates ride-alongs as "a great way for community members to get to know law enforcement officers" |
| **TONE** | positive, encouraging, pointing out the benefits of ride-alongs, using positive words like *great* and *wonderful* |
| **STRUCTURE** | descriptive: describes ride-alongs, giving specific examples to support the argument that they are valuable |

## Examples

**6. Author's Purpose**

Several law enforcement departments in the United States have implemented sUAS (small unmanned aircraft systems), or drone programs. Drones provide intelligence, surveillance, and reconnaissance, known as ISR, helping inform decision-makers in reconstructing accidents and crime scenes, finding victims in search and rescue, and managing fire scenes. Local jurisdictions, such as the Los Angeles County Sheriff's Department, use drones. So do federal agencies like the US Border Patrol. What was once a military tool is becoming a valuable resource for law enforcement.

What is the purpose of this passage?

(A) to argue that drones are important for patrol
(B) to explain the history of drones in law enforcement
(C) to persuade readers that drone programs should be funded
(D) to describe how drones are used by law enforcement agencies

**7. Point of View**

Any law enforcement officer should expect to use force on the job at some point. Fortunately, officers have many nonlethal options for controlling a suspect or situation. Tasers, pepper spray, and batons are all effective for neutralizing a threat in many circumstances. Officers also train in basic ground and hand-to-hand tactics, though if possible they should avoid physical encounters for safety reasons. However, in certain situations officers must use their service pistols, which may result in a fatality.

Which of the following BEST describes what the author believes?

(A) Most forms of nonlethal force are effective, but not all.
(B) Lethal force should never be used because it is unethical.
(C) Officers should use nonlethal force if possible.
(D) Physical encounters should always be avoided.

**8. Tone**

Managing people is complicated in any field, and law enforcement is no different. Managers must balance administrative, financial, disciplinary, and policy responsibilities. Good managers also need to be aware of their subordinates' mental health in stressful fields like law enforcement. Recognizing the signs of stress, depression, substance abuse, and afflictions like post-traumatic stress disorder (PTSD) is an important skill for those who manage law enforcement personnel. The department can provide officers with support for mental wellness, improving their job performance and safety. The sooner a supervisor can spot symptoms, the faster the officer can receive assistance.

Which of the following best describes the author's attitude toward officers' mental health?

(A) dismissive
(B) sympathetic
(C) pitying
(D) angry

9. **Text Structure**

Increasingly, police departments require law enforcement officers to wear body cameras when they interact with members of the public. Some officers agree with this policy because the cameras provide protection against false complaints of police misconduct. Footage can exonerate police officers, proving their professionalism in situations. Other officers are cautious, worried that the cameras could limit officer discretion. Their concern is that supervisors might review and second-guess the officers' decisions during a call. What is undeniable is that the trend of body cameras is not going away as more jurisdictions across America adopt them.

What is the structure of this text?

**(A)** cause and effect

**(B)** order and sequence

**(C)** problem and solution

**(D)** compare and contrast

# Comparing Passages

Sometimes readers need to compare and contrast two texts. After reading and identifying the main idea of each text, look for similarities and differences in the main idea, details, claims, evidence, characters, and so on.

When answering questions about two texts, first identify whether the question is about a similarity or a difference. Then look for specific details in the text that connect to the answers. After that, determine which answer choice best describes the similarity or difference.

> Use a Venn diagram, table, or highlighters to organize similarities and differences between texts.

Table 1.5. Comparing Passages

**INTRANASALLY ADMINISTERED NALOXONE**

Because even tiny amounts of the dangerous narcotic Fentanyl can result in overdose or death, many law enforcement officers carry the anti-overdose drug naloxone in case they encounter the frequently abused substance. Naloxone can be administered intranasally, allowing for rapid absorption into the bloodstream. The rescuer lays the victim on his or her back and sprays the medication into one nostril. The rescuer needs minimal training to administer naloxone in this way.

**INJECTABLE NALOXONE**

Naloxone, a medication that counteracts opioid overdose, is carried by many law enforcement officers in case of accidental contact with powerful narcotics like Fentanyl. Naloxone must be injected by trained first responders. Injectable naloxone is effective when the nasal cavity is damaged, for instance, if the victim has head trauma. Injectable naloxone is also used on detection dogs that have accidentally inhaled Fentanyl or another opioid and need a lower dose of naloxone than a human would.

| | |
|---|---|
| **SIMILARITIES (COMPARISON)** | Both substances are used by law enforcement to fight accidental opioid overdose. |
| **DIFFERENCES (CONTRAST)** | Intranasally administered naloxone works rapidly and can be given by anyone. Injectable naloxone must be administered by a trained first responder and is more effective in specific situations. |

**Example**

10. **Comparing Passages**

    Self-Driving Cars: A Safer America

    Self-driving cars, already present on our streets, are the wave of the future. They will make roads safer. Unlike human drivers, self-driving cars don't drink and drive, get lost in conversation, or fumble with phones. They can also be programmed to strictly adhere to the speed limit and traffic laws. That makes them the best bet for road and highway safety. Law enforcement officials will have more time to pursue violent criminals if they don't need to spend as much time monitoring highways for speeders and unsafe drivers.

    The Dangers of Autonomous Vehicles

    Many people are excited about autonomous vehicles, or self-driving cars, but they are risky machines. Already, several have been involved in deadly accidents, failing to brake for pedestrians or making inappropriate turns resulting in wrecks. Autonomous vehicles can malfunction; they occupy a gray area for law enforcement. What if an autonomous vehicle is speeding? How can highway patrol pull it over? What is the role for the traffic officer in an accident caused by a self-driving car? Who is accountable? There is no substitution for an experienced human driver with good judgment.

    Which of these statements BEST compares the information in both texts?

    **(A)** Autonomous vehicles are a social advantage.

    **(B)** People are already using self-driving cars.

    **(C)** Self-driving cars occupy a legal gray area.

    **(D)** Officers will benefit from self-driving cars.

# MEANING OF WORDS

To understand the meanings of unfamiliar words, use **CONTEXT CLUES**. Context clues are hints the author provides to help readers define difficult words. They can be found in words or phrases in the same sentence or in a neighboring sentence. Look for synonyms, antonyms, definitions, examples, and explanations in the text to determine the meaning of the unfamiliar word.

Sometimes parts of a word can make its meaning easier to determine. **AFFIXES** are added to **ROOT WORDS** (a word's basic form) to modify meaning. **PREFIXES** are added to the beginning of root words, while **SUFFIXES** are added to the ending. Divide words into parts, finding meaning in each part. Take, for example, the word *unjustifiable*: the prefix is *un–* (*not*), the root word is *justify* ("to prove reasonable"), and the suffix is *–able* (referring to a quality). Affixes are discussed in more detail in chapter 2.

Use what you know about a word to figure out its meaning, then look for clues in the sentence or paragraph.

Another way to determine the meaning of unknown words is to consider their denotation and connotation with other words in the sentence. **DENOTATION** is the literal meaning of a word, while **CONNOTATION** is the positive or negative associations of a word.

Authors use words to convey thoughts, but the meaning may be different from a literal meaning of the words. This is called **FIGURATIVE LANGUAGE**. Types of figurative language include similes, metaphors, hyperboles, and personification.

Similes compare two things that are not alike with the words *like* or *as*. Metaphors are used to compare two things that are not exactly alike but may share a certain characteristic.

Hyperboles are statements that exaggerate something to make a point or to draw attention to a certain feature. Personification involves using human characteristics to describe an animal or object.

Table 1.6. Meanings of Words

Check fraud used to be a major crime, but today fewer people than ever use paper checks. Still, criminals continue to find ways to steal from consumers. Identity theft is a threat to all Americans as more people use credit cards and electronic financial applications than cash. Despite encryption techniques that protect personal details, computer hackers periodically uncover consumers' financial information in security breaches. Small-time thieves steal credit cards, use card skimmers at gas stations, or make fake cards with specialized machines.

| | |
|---|---|
| **CONTEXT CLUES** | Techniques *protect* personal details; the details are still *uncovered* for criminal use. |
| **AFFIXES** | The prefix *en–* in *encryption* means *cause to*. The suffix *–ion* suggests an act or process. |
| **ROOTS** | The root of the word *encryption* is *crypt*, which means *hide* or *conceal*. |
| **MEANING** | *Encryption* means "the process of causing something to be hidden." |

## Examples

**11. Context Clues**

After a few high-profile missing-persons cases in the 1970s and 1980s, parents in many communities became concerned about "stranger danger." Families worried that their children would be <u>abducted</u>, taken by criminal outsiders. However, when a child goes missing, the perpetrator is usually someone the child knows. Family members make up the majority of perpetrators in cases of missing children. It is very rare that a child is kidnapped by a total stranger, though it can happen.

What does *abducted* mean as it is used in the passage?

**(A)** taken by criminal outsiders

**(B)** the perpetrator

**(C)** family members make up

**(D)** "stranger danger"

**12. Root Words and Affixes**

Unfortunately, automobile accidents happen. The good news is, most result in only minor damage to vehicles. Still, drivers are responsible for calling the police and reporting the incident, regardless of its severity. An officer will arrive to take the statement of each driver and survey the scene. The officer will closely examine the drivers' behavior and mannerisms to determine if their claims are <u>credible</u>. After all the evidence is collected, reviewed, and approved, the insurance company assigns blame to one party. The officer's role is key in this determination.

Based on affixes and context clues, what does *credible* mean?

**(A)** believable

**(B)** achievable

**(C)** likeable

**(D)** noticeable

### 13. Figurative Language

Nothing in the world is harder than waking up for a job you don't love. Who wants to drag themselves to work every day? That's why it's important to follow your passions. Many say that serving the public in law enforcement is more than just a job; it's a calling. Police officers risk their lives to serve and protect the public. It takes a certain kind of person to thrive in law enforcement.

Which type of figurative language is used in the second sentence?

**(A)** simile

**(B)** metaphor

**(C)** personification

**(D)** hyperbole

# Answer Key

1. **(B) Correct.** The topic of the passage is police dogs. The passage mentions how long they work, their handlers, and the usual retirement circumstances of police dogs as supporting ideas.

2. **(D) Correct.** The author writes that "the allied tribes...decisively defeated their US foes," and the remainder of the passage provides details to support this idea.

3. **(C) Correct.** The passage specifically presents this detail as one of the advantages of subcontracting services.

4. **(B) Correct.** The statement "The driver was performing unsafe maneuvers" is a judgment about the safety of the actions taken by the driver. The driver (or his attorney) might argue that his driving was safe.

5. **(D) Correct.** The passage states that swatting is dangerous because of confusion caused by false information and the nature of a violent raid. The sentence "Tragic outcomes are not uncommon" suggests that injury or death can happen.

6. **(D) Correct.** The text provides details on how drones are used and what departments use them.

7. **(C) Correct.** The author discusses many options for nonlethal force, using the word *fortunately* to show a preference for it. However, the author also allows that lethal force is sometimes necessary.

8. **(B) Correct.** The author states that "[t]he department can provide officers with support" and that supervisors should "be aware of their subordinates' mental health." By taking these positions, the author is being sympathetic and supportive of officers' mental health.

9. **(D) Correct.** In this text, two perspectives on body cameras are compared and contrasted.

10. **(B) Correct.** Both passages indicate that self-driving cars, or autonomous vehicles, are already in use.

11. **(A) Correct.** The phrase "taken by criminal outsiders" redefines the word *abducted* in the sentence.

12. **(A) Correct.** The root *cred* means *believe*. The words *evidence, reviewed,* and *approved* are context clues hinting that something needs to be believed and accepted.

13. **(B) Correct.** The writer uses the metaphor *drag*. No one literally drags himself or herself to work.

# WRITING

## INTRODUCTION

Written and verbal communications are equally important in law enforcement. Writing accurate, clear, and concise memos, warrants, and police reports ensures that the information provided is as the officer intended. Unclear or confusing verbal communication can create misunderstanding and even danger if an officer is attempting to control a volatile situation. The same is true of written work. Wordy, incoherent, error-laden communications create confusion.

Most police exams specifically test three aspects of writing: clarity, vocabulary, and spelling.

Clear and concise writing helps readers easily understand a message. In law enforcement, the last thing an officer wishes is for lawyers, juries, or the public to have to *guess* what he or she meant in a report or other written communication. Cases have been won and lost based on officer testimony related to a well-written or poorly written report.

Inspect the following two passages as an example of how wordiness and grammatical errors can confuse communication.

> **PASSAGE ONE**
>
> On Friday, August 17, 2014, about 1530 hours while working as a patrol officer in full uniform in Sector 2 of River City I heard over my car radio that Officer Smith had two people in front of Superior Court with warrants. I arrived at the Superior Court and met with Officer Smith. Officer Smith told me a woman, identified as Jane Johnson, and a man, identified as Ronald Jones, were at the courthouse. Jane and Ronald were at the court for a family hearing.
>
> A records check with River City Records and Warrants confirmed Jane had a misdemeanor warrant, and Ronald had a felony warrant, out of River City.
>
> Jane and Ronald were arrested without incident to answer for the warrant.

> **PASSAGE TWO**
>
> On Friday, August 17, 2014, about 1530 hours I contacted Jane Johnson and Ronald Jones in front of the River City Superior Court. Jane and Ronald were at the court for a family hearing. I had information both parties had active warrants for their arrest.
>
> A records check with River City Records and Warrants confirmed Jane had an active misdemeanor warrant for her arrest and Ronald had an active felony warrant for his arrest, both issued by River City.
>
> I arrested Jane and Ronald without incident to answer for their warrants.

Isn't it much easier to understand passage two? Are the sentences clear, concise, and grammatically correct, and do they contain all the necessary information? On the other hand, does passage one seem wordy and filled with grammatical errors? Is it clear or confusing? Unclear reports of search warrants could lead to poor investigations, arrests, and prosecutions.

Many police exams test only common grammatical mistakes. Knowing the rules of grammar, mechanics, and sentence structure will help you succeed. Furthermore, avoiding common errors can help add clarity to your written communication. We review the basics and common mistakes in this chapter.

Police exams also frequently ask you to define and spell words. Two sections of this chapter focus on building your vocabulary, determining the meaning of unfamiliar words, and reviewing spelling rules.

## THE PARTS OF SPEECH

**NOUNS** are the words that describe people, places, things, and ideas. The subject of a sentence is typically a noun. For example, in the sentence "The station was very clean," the subject, *station*, is a noun; it is a place.

Nouns have several subcategories: common nouns (*chair, car, house*), proper nouns (*Julie, David*), noncountable nouns (*money, water*), and countable nouns (*dollars, cubes*), among others. There is much crossover among these subcategories (for example, *chair* is both common and countable), and other subcategories do exist.

> **SINGULAR PRONOUNS**
> • I, me, my, mine
> • you, your, yours
> • he, him, his
> • she, her, hers
> • it, its
> **PLURAL PRONOUNS**
> • we, us, our, ours
> • they, them, their, theirs

**PRONOUNS** replace nouns in a sentence or paragraph, allowing a writer to achieve a smooth flow throughout a text by avoiding unnecessary repetition. While there are countless nouns in the English language, there are only a few types of pronouns. Take the sentence "Sam stayed home from school because Sam was not feeling well." The noun *Sam* appears twice in the same sentence. Instead, the pronoun *he* can be used to stand in for *Sam*: "Sam stayed home from school because he was not feeling well."

**VERBS** express action (*run, jump, play*) or state of being (*is, seems*). Verbs that describe action are **ACTION VERBS**, and those that describe being are **LINKING VERBS**.

ACTION: My brother <u>plays</u> tennis.

LINKING: He is the best player on the team.

**ADJECTIVES** provide more information about a noun in a sentence. Take the sentence "The boy hit the ball." If you want your readers to know more about the noun *boy*, you could use an adjective to describe him: *the little boy, the young boy, the tall boy.*

**ADVERBS** describe verbs, adjectives, and even other adverbs. For example, in the sentence "The doctor had recently hired a new employee," the adverb *recently* tells us more about how the action *hired* took place.

> Participles are nouns or adjectives formed by adding *–ed* or *–ing* to a verb.
> <u>Seated</u> politely, Ron listened to his friend's boring story.
> Maya petted the <u>sleeping</u> cat.

**PREPOSITIONS** express the location of a noun or pronoun in relation to other words and phrases described in a sentence. For example, in the sentence "The nurse parked her car in a parking garage," the preposition *in* describes the position of the car in relation to the garage. Together, the preposition and the noun that follow it are called a **PREPOSITIONAL PHRASE**. In this example, the prepositional phrase is *in a parking garage*.

**CONJUNCTIONS** connect words, phrases, and clauses. **INTERJECTIONS**, like *wow* and *hey*, express emotion and are most commonly used in conversation and casual writing.

**Examples**

1. Which of the following lists includes all the nouns in the following sentence?
   I have lived in Minnesota since August, but I still don't own a warm coat or gloves.
   - **(A)** coat, gloves
   - **(B)** I, coat, gloves
   - **(C)** Minnesota, August, coat, gloves
   - **(D)** I, Minnesota, August, warm, coat, gloves

2. Which of the following lists includes all the adjectives in the following sentence?
   The new chef carefully stirred the boiling soup and then lowered the heat.
   - **(A)** new, boiling
   - **(B)** new, carefully, boiling
   - **(C)** new, carefully, boiling, heat
   - **(D)** new, carefully, boiling, lowered, heat

3. Choose the word that best completes the sentence.
   Her love _____ blueberry muffins kept her coming back to the bakery every week.
   - **(A)** to
   - **(B)** with
   - **(C)** of
   - **(D)** about

# Punctuation

The basic rules for using the major punctuation marks are given in the table below.

Table 2.1. Using Punctuation

| PUNCTUATION | PURPOSE | EXAMPLE |
|---|---|---|
| Period | Ending sentences | Periods go at the end of complete sentences. |
| Question mark | Ending questions | What's the best way to end a sentence? |
| Exclamation point | Ending sentences that show extreme emotion | I'll never understand how to use commas! |
| Comma | Joining two independent clauses (always with a coordinating conjunction) | Commas can be used to join clauses, but they must always be followed by a coordinating conjunction. |
| Comma | Setting apart introductory and nonessential words and phrases | Commas, when used properly, set apart extra information in a sentence. |
| Comma | Separating items in a list | My favorite punctuation marks include the colon, semicolon, and period. |
| Semicolon | Joining together two independent clauses (never used with a conjunction) | I love exclamation points; they make sentences seem so exciting! |
| Colon | Introducing a list, explanation, or definition | When I see a colon, I know what to expect: more information. |
| Apostrophe | Forming contractions | It's amazing how many people can't use apostrophes correctly. |
| Apostrophe | Showing possession | Parentheses are my sister's favorite punctuation; she finds commas' rules confusing. |
| Quotation marks | Indicating a direct quote | I said to her, "Tell me more about parentheses." |

**Examples**

4. Which of the following sentences contains an error in punctuation?
   - (A) I love apple pie! John exclaimed with a smile.
   - (B) Jennifer loves Adam's new haircut.
   - (C) Billy went to the store; he bought bread, milk, and cheese.
   - (D) Alexandra hates raisins, but she loves chocolate chips.

5. Sam, do you want to come with us for dinner_
   Which punctuation mark correctly completes the sentence?
   - (A) .
   - (B) ?
   - (C) ;
   - (D) :

## PHRASES

Understanding subjects and predicates is key to understanding what a phrase is. The **SUBJECT** is what the sentence is about; the **PREDICATE** contains the verb and its modifiers.

> The nurse at the front desk will answer any questions you have.
>
> **SUBJECT**: the nurse at the front desk
>
> **PREDICATE**: will answer any questions you have

A **PHRASE** is a group of words that communicates only part of an idea because it lacks either a subject or a predicate. Phrases can begin with prepositions, verbs, nouns, or participles.

> **PREPOSITIONAL PHRASE**: The dog is hiding <u>under the porch</u>.
>
> **VERB PHRASE**: The chef <u>wanted to cook</u> a different dish.
>
> **NOUN PHRASE**: <u>The big red barn</u> rests beside <u>the vacant chicken house</u>.
>
> **PARTICIPIAL PHRASE**: <u>Walking quietly</u>, she tried not to wake the baby.

### Example

6. Identify the type of phrase underlined in the following sentence:

   The experienced paraprofessional worked independently <u>with the eager students</u>.

   **(A)** prepositional phrase

   **(B)** noun phrase

   **(C)** verb phrase

   **(D)** participial phrase

## CLAUSES

**CLAUSES** contain both a subject and a predicate. They can be either independent or dependent. An **INDEPENDENT** (or main) **CLAUSE** can stand alone as its own sentence.

> The dog ate her homework.

**DEPENDENT** (or subordinate) **CLAUSES** cannot stand alone as their own sentences. They start with a subordinating conjunction, relative pronoun, or relative adjective, which will make them sound incomplete.

> <u>Because</u> the dog ate her homework

Clauses can be joined together to create more complex sentences. **COORDINATING CONJUNCTIONS** join two independent clauses, and **SUBORDINATING CONJUNCTIONS** join an independent to a dependent clause.

Table 2.2. Conjunctions

| Coordinating | for, and, nor, but, or, yet, so (FANBOYS) | The nurse prepared the patient for surgery, <u>and</u> the doctor performed the surgery. |
|---|---|---|
| Subordinating | after, although, because, if, since, so that, though, until, when, while | She had to ride the subway <u>because</u> her car was being serviced. |

### Example

7. Choose the word that best completes the sentence.

   Christine left her house early on Monday morning, _____ she was still late for work.

   **(A)** but
   **(B)** and
   **(C)** for
   **(D)** or

# Common Grammatical Errors

## Pronoun-Antecedent Agreement

Pronouns must agree with their ANTECEDENTS (the words they replace) in number; however, some pronouns also require gender agreement (*him, her*). PRONOUN-ANTECEDENT AGREEMENT rules can be found below:

1. Antecedents joined by *and* typically require a plural pronoun.
   The <u>children and their dogs</u> enjoyed <u>their</u> day at the beach.
   If the two nouns refer to the same person, a singular pronoun is preferable.
   <u>My best friend and confidant</u> still lives in <u>her</u> log cabin.

2. For compound antecedents joined by *or*, the pronoun agrees with the nearer or nearest antecedent.
   Either the resident mice <u>or the manager's cat</u> gets <u>itself</u> a meal of good leftovers.

3. When indefinite pronouns function in a sentence, the pronoun must agree with the number of the indefinite pronoun.
   <u>Neither</u> student finished <u>his or her</u> assignment.
   <u>Both</u> students finished <u>their</u> assignments.

4. When collective nouns function as antecedents, the pronoun choice will be singular or plural depending on the function of the collective.
   The <u>audience</u> was cheering as <u>it</u> rose to <u>its</u> feet in unison.
   Our <u>family</u> are spending <u>their</u> vacations in Maine, Hawaii, and Rome.

5. When *each* and *every* precede the antecedent, the pronoun agreement will be singular.
   <u>Each and every man, woman, and child</u> brings unique qualities to <u>his or her</u> family.
   <u>Every creative writer, technical writer, and research writer</u> is attending <u>his or her</u> assigned lecture.

How would you complete the following sentence? "Every boy and girl should check _____ homework before turning it in." Many people would use the pronoun *their*. But since the antecedent is "every boy and girl," technically, the correct answer would be *his or her*. Using *they* or *their* in similar situations is increasingly accepted in formal speech, however. It is unlikely that you will see questions like this on a police exam, but if you do, it is safest to use the technically correct response.

### Example

8. In which of the following sentences do the nouns and pronouns NOT agree?
   - **(A)** After we walked inside, we took off our hats and shoes and hung them in the closet.
   - **(B)** The members of the band should leave her instruments in the rehearsal room.
   - **(C)** The janitor on duty should rinse out his or her mop before leaving for the day.
   - **(D)** When you see someone in trouble, you should always try to help them.

### Vague or Unclear Pronouns

A vague or unclear reference is generally the result of a **PRONOUN ERROR**. Pronoun errors occur when it is not clear what the antecedent of a pronoun is—the word it replaces. In the first sentence below, it is difficult to determine whose notes the officer gave to the Assistant District Attorney. Do the notes belong to the officer or to the ADA? The antecedent of the pronoun *his* is unclear. To improve this sentence, be sure the pronoun refers to only one antecedent noun.

> **WRONG:** Officer Lane gave Assistant District Attorney Poole <u>his</u> notes.
>
> **CORRECT:** Officer Lane gave <u>his</u> notes to Assistant District Attorney Poole.

Another way to ensure clarity in writing is to avoid using pronouns to refer to an implied idea; it is better to state the idea explicitly. In the sentence below, the writer misuses the pronoun *it*. The reader might be confused: did jury deliberation take a long time, or did the process of the trial take a long time? To improve this sentence, the writer should state the idea explicitly, avoiding a pronoun altogether.

> **WRONG:** The jury reached a verdict in the defendant's case, but <u>it</u> took a long time.
>
> **CORRECT:** The jury reached a verdict in the defendant's case, but <u>the deliberations</u> took a long time.

### Example

9. Choose the more clearly written sentence.
   - **(A)** John said he and Frank were fighting when he was shot.
   - **(B)** John said he and Frank were fighting when Frank was shot.

## Subject-Verb Agreement

Verbs are conjugated to indicate PERSON, which refers to the point of view of the sentence. First person is the speaker (*I, we*); second person is the person being addressed (*you*); and third person is outside the conversation (*they, them*). Verbs are also conjugated to match the NUMBER (singular or plural) of their subject. HELPING VERBS (*to be, to have, to do*) are used to conjugate verbs. An unconjugated verb is called an INFINITIVE and includes the word *to* in front of it (*to be, to break*).

Table 2.3. Verb Conjugation (Present Tense)

| PERSON | SINGULAR | PLURAL |
| --- | --- | --- |
| First person | I give | we give |
| Second person | you give | you (all) give |
| Third person | he/she/it gives | they give |

Ignore words between the subject and the verb when trying to match a subject and verb:
The new library ~~with its many books and rooms~~ fills a long-felt need.

Verbs must agree in number with their subjects. (In some other languages, such as Spanish, verbs must also agree with their subjects in gender.) SUBJECT-VERB AGREEMENT rules follow:

1. Singular subjects agree with singular verbs; plural subjects agree with plural verbs.
   The girl walks her dog.
   The girls walk their dogs.

2. Compound subjects joined by *and* typically take a plural verb unless they are considered one item.
   Correctness and precision are required for all good writing.
   Macaroni and cheese makes a great snack for children.

3. Compound subjects joined by *or* or *nor* agree with the nearer or nearest subject.
   Neither I nor my friends are looking forward to our final exams.
   Neither my friends nor I am looking forward to our final exams.

4. All singular indefinite pronouns agree with singular verbs.
   Neither of the students is happy about the play.
   Each of the many cars is on the grass.
   Every one of the administrators speaks highly of Officer Larkin.

5. All plural indefinite pronouns agree with plural verbs.
   Several of the students are happy about the play.
   Both of the cars are on the grass.
   Many of the administrators speak highly of Officer Larkin.

6. Some of the singular indefinite pronouns (*all, most, some, more, any*) change agreement depending on the object of the preposition.
   All of the pie is gone.
   All of the pies are gone.
   Some of the bucket is dirty.
   Some of the buckets are dirty.

7. Collective nouns agree with singular verbs when the collective acts as one unit. Collective nouns agree with plural verbs when the collective acts as individuals within the group.

The <u>jury announces</u> its decision after sequestration. (*They act as one unit.*)
The <u>jury make</u> phone calls during their break time. (*They act as individuals.*)

8. Nouns that are plural in form but singular in meaning will agree with singular verbs.
   <u>Measles is</u> a painful disease.
   <u>Sixty dollars is</u> too much to pay for that book.

9. Singular verbs come after titles, business corporations, and words used as terms.
   <u>"Three Little Kittens" is</u> a favorite nursery rhyme for many children.
   <u>General Motors is</u> a major employer for the city.

### Example

10. Which of the following sentences contains a subject-verb error?
    - **(A)** The witness and her mother are asked to remain seated.
    - **(B)** Some of the officers at the station is planning to stay late.
    - **(C)** My partner and I are happy with the new schedule.
    - **(D)** The department is hiring for many new positions this year.

### Verb Tense Agreement

Verbs are also conjugated to indicate TENSE, or when the action has happened. Actions can happen in the past, present, or future. Tense also describes over how long a period the action took place.

- **SIMPLE** verbs describe general truths or something that happened once.
- **CONTINUOUS** verbs describe an ongoing action.
- **PERFECT** verbs describe repeated actions or actions that started in the past and have been completed.
- **PERFECT CONTINUOUS** verbs describe actions that started in the past and are continuing.

Table 2.4. Verb Tenses

| TENSE | PAST | PRESENT | FUTURE |
| --- | --- | --- | --- |
| Simple | I <u>gave</u> her a gift yesterday. | I <u>give</u> her a gift every day. | I <u>will give</u> her a gift on her birthday. |
| Continuous | I <u>was giving</u> her a gift when you got here. | I <u>am giving</u> her a gift; come in! | I <u>will be giving</u> her a gift at dinner. |
| Perfect | I <u>had given</u> her a gift before you got there. | I <u>have given</u> her a gift already. | I <u>will have given</u> her a gift by midnight. |
| Perfect continuous | Her friends <u>had been giving</u> her gifts all night when I arrived. | I <u>have been giving</u> her gifts every year for nine years. | I <u>will have been giving</u> her gifts on holidays for ten years next year. |

The verb tenses in a sentence must agree with each other and with the other information provided in the sentence. Pay attention to words like *before, after, tomorrow, yesterday, then,* and *next*, which describe when in time events occurred.

> **WRONG:** After he changed clothes, the officer will be ready to go home.
>
> **CORRECT:** After he changed clothes, the officer was ready to go home.

In the example above, the introductory phrase describes an action that was completed in the past (*he changed*), so the rest of the sentence should also be in the past (*was ready*).

### Example

11. Which verb phrase best completes the sentence?
    By this time tomorrow, we _____ in New York.
    - **(A)** will have arrived
    - **(B)** have arrived
    - **(C)** arrive
    - **(D)** was arriving

## Comparing Adjectives and Adverbs

The suffix *–er* is used when comparing two things, and the suffix *–est* is used when comparing more than two. Adjectives longer than two syllables are compared using *more* (for two things) or *most* (for three or more things).

> Anne is taller than Steve, but Steve is more coordinated.
>
> Of the five brothers, Billy is the funniest, and Alex is the most intelligent.

*More* and *most* should NOT be used in conjunction with *–er* and *–est* endings.

> **WRONG:** My most warmest sweater is made of wool.
>
> **CORRECT:** My warmest sweater is made of wool.

### Example

12. Which of the following sentences contains an adjective error?
    - **(A)** The new red car was faster than the old blue car.
    - **(B)** Reggie's apartment is in the tallest building on the block.
    - **(C)** The slice of cake was tastier than the brownie.
    - **(D)** Of the four speeches, Jerry's was the most long.

## Misplaced Modifiers

A **MODIFIER** is a word or phrase—like an adjective—that adds detail to a sentence. Adjectives, adverbs, and modifying phrases should be placed as close as possible to the word they modify. **MISPLACED MODIFIERS** can create confusing or nonsensical sentences.

> **WRONG:** Running down the alley, the siren sounded and the police officer knew backup had arrived.
>
> **CORRECT:** Running down the alley, the police officer heard the siren and knew backup had arrived.

In the first example above, the phrase "running down the alley" looks like it is modifying "the siren." For clarity, it should be placed next to "the police officer," the noun it modifies.

> **WRONG:** Describing the crime, the jury listened to the prosecutor deliver his opening statement.
>
> **CORRECT:** The jury listened to the prosecutor deliver his opening statement describing the crime.

In this example, the phrase "describing the crime" is first placed next to the word "jury," making it seem like the jury is describing the crime. To fix the sentence, the modifier should be moved so it is clear that the prosecutor is describing the crime.

### Example

13. Choose the more clearly written sentence.
    - **(A)** During police contacts, failure to follow directions is often the cause of officer uses of force.
    - **(B)** During police contacts, failure to follow directions often is the cause of officer uses of force.

## Sentence Fragments

A sentence fragment occurs when a group of words is followed by a period but does not form a complete sentence or thought. A sentence fragment can be corrected by turning it into a complete sentence that has at least one independent clause.

> **WRONG:** Because he was tired of presiding over cases involving the same criminals in his courtroom.
>
> **CORRECT:** The judge left the bench because he was tired of presiding over cases involving the same criminals in his courtroom.

### Example

14. Choose the more clearly written sentence.
    - **(A)** The suspect robbed an elderly woman and then fled the scene in a red sedan heading northbound on Eighth Avenue.
    - **(B)** The suspect robbed an elderly woman and then fled the scene in a red sedan. Heading northbound on Eighth Avenue.

## Run-on Sentences

A **RUN-ON SENTENCE** is two or more complete sentences not separated by appropriate punctuation, such as a comma, period, or semicolon. For example, the following is a run-on sentence: "Jack shot his friend Mark over a pool game, Jack was mad because he thought Mark was cheating."

Be sure to separate each complete thought with proper punctuation. Applying this rule changes the preceding sentence: "Jack shot his friend Mark over a pool game. Jack was mad because he thought Mark was cheating."

> **Example**
>
> 15. Choose the more clearly written sentence.
>     - **(A)** Jane broke into the house intending to steal items to exchange for drugs she activated the alarm and ran away.
>     - **(B)** Jane broke into the house intending to steal items to exchange for drugs. She activated the alarm and ran away.

## VOCABULARY

Vocabulary is a collection of words used or known in language. Possessing a large vocabulary can help you better understand communications. It can improve your ability to determine context and add clarity to the written or spoken word. Law enforcement vocabulary can be very technical, but it also contains many commonly used words. Most police officer exams measure your ability to understand and appropriately use *common* words.

Developing a large vocabulary takes time and practice; it cannot be done overnight. However, studying commonly used words and their synonyms can help. Synonyms are words that share the same or nearly the same meaning as other words. Understanding word roots, prefixes, suffixes, and how they affect words can also help you determine the meaning of unfamiliar words based on the word's structure.

### Root Words

A **ROOT WORD** is the base of a word. It comes after a prefix or before a suffix. In English, many root words come from ancient Greek and Latin. Root words hold meaning and can stand alone as words. Learning to recognize common root words can help you build your vocabulary and make educated guesses about unfamiliar words. It can also help improve your ability to comprehend various types of communications.

Table 2.5 lists some common root words, their meanings, and examples.

Table 2.5. Common Root Words

| ROOT | MEANING | EXAMPLES |
| --- | --- | --- |
| *actus, act* | drive, lead, act | active, action, activate, react |
| *acurer* | to sharpen | acute, acumen, acuity |
| *agon* | contest, struggle | antagonist, agony |
| *ambi* | both | ambiguous, ambidextrous |
| *anthropo* | man, human, humanity | anthropologist, philanthropist |
| *aqua* | water | aquarium, aquatic |
| *arbit* | judge | arbitrary, arbitration |
| *archos, arch* | chief, first, rule | monarch, archangel, anarchy |
| *aud* | to hear | audience, audible, auditory |
| *auto* | self | autobiography, autograph, autoimmune, automobile |
| *bene* | good | benevolent, beneficial |
| *bio* | life | biology, biography |

| ROOT | MEANING | EXAMPLES |
| --- | --- | --- |
| capere, cip, cept | take, seize | captive, capture, captivate, intercept |
| cedere, ced | to go, yield | recede, precede, exceed, predecessor |
| chron | time | chronological, chronic, synchronize |
| circum | around | circumference, circumvent, circumscribe |
| clino, clin | lean, slant | incline, decline, inclination, recline |
| contra, counter | against | contradict, contrary, counteract |
| cred | believe | creed, incredible |
| crit | judge | criticize, critical |
| crypto, crypt | hide, conceal | cryptic, cryptogram, encryption |
| dict | to say | dictation, dictate, predict |
| duc, duct | to lead | conduct, induce, induct |
| dyna | power | dynamic, dynamite, dynamo |
| dys | bad, hard, unlucky | dysfunctional, dyslexic, dystopia |
| equ | equal, even | equidistant, inequity, equivalent, equitable |
| errare, err, errat | wander, go astray | errant, err, erratic, aberration |
| fac | to do, to make | factory, manufacture, artifact |
| finis, fin | end, limit | final, definite, infinite |
| form | shape | conform, reform |
| fort | strength | fortitude, fortress, fortify, comfort |
| fract | to break | fracture, fraction |
| gno, gnos | know | diagnosis, ignore, incognito, cognitive |
| gram | something written | telegram, diagram, grammar |
| graph | writing | graphic, autograph |
| gravis, grav, griev | heavy, serious | grave, grievance, grievous, aggravate, gravity |
| hetero | different | heteronym, heterogeneous |
| homo | same | homonym, homogenous |
| hydro | water | hydrate, dehydrate, hydraulic |
| hypo | below, beneath | hypothermia, hypothetical, hypoglycemic |
| ject | throw | eject, project, reject |
| jud | judge | judicial, prejudice |
| jus, jur, just | right, law, oath | abjure, perjury, conjure, jury, jurisprudence |
| juven | young | juvenile, rejuvenate |
| mal | bad | malfeasance, malevolent, malcontent |
| mater | mother | maternal, maternity |
| meter, metr | measure | thermometer, perimeter, metric |
| micro | small | microbe, microscope, microchip |
| mis, miso | hate, wrong | misanthrope, misogyny, misbehave |
| mono | one | monologue, monotonous, monotheism |

Table 2.5. Common Root Words (continued)

| ROOT | MEANING | EXAMPLES |
|---|---|---|
| morph | form, shape | morphology, metamorphosis |
| mort | death | mortal, mortician, immortal |
| multi | many | multimedia, multiple, multiply, multicolored |
| nym | name | antonym, synonym, homonym |
| onus, oner | burden | onerous, onus, exonerate |
| opsis, optic | sight, eye, view | optical, synopsis |
| pater | father | paternal, paternity |
| phil | love | philanthropist, philosophy |
| phobia | fear | claustrophobia, acrophobia, phobic |
| phon | sound | cacophony, phonetic, symphony |
| photo, phos | light | photograph, photogenic, phosphorous |
| placaere | appease | placate, placid |
| port | to carry | portable, transportation, export |
| pretiare, prec | to value | precious, deprecation, depreciation, appreciation |
| pseudo | false | pseudonym, pseudoscience |
| psycho | soul, spirit | psychology, psychic, psychotic |
| rupt | to break | bankrupt, disrupt, erupt |
| scope | to watch, see | microscope, telescope |
| scrib, scribe | to write | inscribe, prescribe, describe |
| sect, sec | to cut | bisect, section, intersect, dissect |
| sentire, sent | to feel, perceive | consent, resent, sentient, sentiment |
| skep, scop | examine | skeptical, scope |
| spect | to look | inspect, spectator, circumspect, retrospective |
| struct | to build | construct, destruct, restructure, infrastructure |
| tacere, tac, tic | to be silent | tacit, taciturn, reticent |
| techno | art, science, skill | technique, technology |
| tele | far off | television, telephone, teleport |
| tendere | stretch | extend, tend, distend |
| terrere, terr | frighten | deter, terror, terrorism |
| therm | heat | thermal, thermometer, thermos |
| thesis | position | synthesis, hypothesis |
| venire, veni, ven | come, move toward | convention, contravene, intervene |
| vid, vis | to see | video, envision, evident, vision |
| voc | to call | voice, vocalize, advocate |
| zelos | ardor | zeal, zealous, zealot |

## Prefixes

**PREFIXES** are sets of letters that are added to the beginning of a word. Adding a prefix to a word can change its meaning. For instance, if you take the root word *jud*, which means *judge*, and add the prefix *pre–*, which means *before*, you create the word *prejudice*, which means to prejudge.

Prefixes cannot stand on their own as words, but they do hold meaning. Learning to recognize common prefixes builds vocabulary and helps readers make educated guesses about unfamiliar words. It can also help improve reading comprehension in general.

Table 2.6 lists some common prefixes, their meanings, and examples.

Table 2.6. Common Prefixes

| PREFIX | MEANING | EXAMPLES |
| --- | --- | --- |
| *ambi–, amb–* | around, on both sides | ambiguous, ambivalent |
| *anti–* | against, opposite | anticlimactic, antiseptic |
| *bi–* | two | bicycle, bifocals, bilingual |
| *circum–, circa–* | around, about | circumference, circadian, circumvent |
| *com–, con–* | with | communicate, convince |
| *contra–* | against | contradict, contrary, contravene |
| *de–* | reduce, remove | devalue, decelerate, decompose |
| *di, dis–* | not, opposite of | discontinue, disappear, discover, digress |
| *en–, em–* | cause to, into | enact, empower, embrace, enclose |
| *fore–* | before, front of | foreshadow, forebear |
| *il–, im–, in–, ir–* | not, without | illegal, impossible, invalidate, irresponsible |
| *im–, in–* | in, into | import, income |
| *inter–* | between, among | interrupt, intercept, intercede |
| *mid–* | middle | midterm, midway |
| *mis–* | bad, wrong | misinterpret, misspell |
| *non–* | not, without | nonconformist, nonfiction, nonviolent |
| *over–* | excessive | overeat, overconfident |
| *peri–* | around, about | perimeter, periphery |
| *pre–* | before | preexisting, precedent, preview |
| *re–, red–* | again, back, against, behind | recede, redo, retreat, rewrite |
| *semi–* | half, partial | semiconscious, semicircle |
| *sub–* | under | subway, submarine |
| *super–* | above, beyond | superfluous, superhuman, superior |
| *trans–* | across, over, through, beyond | transmit, transgression, transit |
| *un–* | not, opposite of | unusual, unashamed, unfair |

## Suffixes

**SUFFIXES** are the same as prefixes except that suffixes are added to the ends of words rather than the beginnings.

Table 2.7 lists some common suffixes, their meanings, and examples.

Table 2.7. Common Suffixes

| SUFFIX | MEANING | EXAMPLES |
| --- | --- | --- |
| –able, –ible | is, can be | excitable, moveable, collectible |
| –al, –ial | having characteristics of, pertaining to | facial, procedural, universal |
| –cide, –cidum | kill | homicide, insecticide |
| –ed | past tense | arrested, called, treated |
| –en | made of, to cause to be | awaken, frighten, weaken |
| –er, –or | a person who | pioneer, professor, volunteer |
| –er | more | taller, meaner, shorter |
| –est | the most | fastest, meanest, shortest |
| –ful | full of | helpful, shameful, thankful |
| –ic | relating to, having characteristics of | poetic, dogmatic, organic |
| –ing | present participles, materials | sleeping, eating, bedding, frosting |
| –ion, –tion, –ation, –sion | act, process | submission, celebration, navigation |
| –ity, –cy –ty | state of, condition | activity, civility, normalcy, society |
| –ive, –ative, –itive | quality of | active, qualitative, sensitive |
| –ize | to make (forms verb) | compartmentalize, mechanize |
| –less | without | blameless, homeless, remorseless |
| –ly | in the manner of | bravely, courageously, horrifically |
| –ment | state of being, act of | contentment, placement, resentment |
| –ness | state of, condition of | weakness, kindness |
| –ology | study | biology, physiology, sociology |
| –ous, –eous, –ious | having qualities of, full of | riotous, hazardous, righteous, gracious |
| –y | characterized by | sassy, cheeky, slimy |

### Examples

*In the following questions, choose the word from the answer choices that is closest in meaning to the underlined word.*

16. The suspect did not have any OUTSTANDING warrants.
    (A) inactive
    (B) unsettled
    (C) unconfirmed
    (D) confirmed

17. Because a career in law enforcement can be dangerous, officers should not become COMPLACENT.
    (A) confident
    (B) unsafe
    (C) self-satisfied
    (D) cheerful

18. During her testimony, the witness RECANTED her statement.
    (A) affirmed
    (B) rescinded
    (C) retold
    (D) regretted

19. The jury did not believe the suspect's mother was a CREDIBLE witness.
    (A) trustworthy
    (B) likeable
    (C) suitable
    (D) useful

20. The suspect's account of the incident was full of DISCREPANCIES.
    (A) falsities
    (B) inaccuracies
    (C) deception
    (D) inconsistencies

# Spelling

Why is spelling important in law enforcement? Much of what officers write is by hand, at least initially. What's more, any notes or other material an officer writes in connection with a crime or criminal investigation is *discoverable*. That means the court can compel an officer to turn over his or her notes and communications to the court and lawyers for both sides. Right or wrong, spelling could affect the officer's credibility and competence in the eyes of a jury. Many people believe multiple spelling and grammatical errors show a lack of attention to detail and a tendency toward sloppy work. Both are detrimental to effective police work.

Some police officer exams do test on spelling. Thankfully, spelling is the easiest part of the examination to study for. And while you could relegate yourself to simply repetitively writing random words on a piece of paper like you did after school when you were in trouble with the teacher, there are more focused methods to improve your performance on a multiple-choice spelling test. It can help to learn the following tips, tricks, and rules to prevent common spelling errors.

### Homophones

HOMOPHONES are words that sound alike but are spelled differently and hold different meanings, such as *break* and *brake*.

> Officer Brady stepped on the brake to stop the car.
> Officer Brady took a lunch break during his shift.

Commonly confused words include:

- **ACCEPT**: agree
  **EXCEPT**: not including
- **ALOUD**: said out loud
  **ALLOWED**: able to
- **BARE**: uncovered
  **BEAR**: large animal; to carry
- **BRAKE**: to stop
  **BREAK**: to damage or interrupt
- **DIE**: to no longer be alive
  **DYE**: to artificially change color
- **EFFECT**: result (noun)
  **AFFECT**: to change (verb)
- **FLOUR**: used for cooking
  **FLOWER**: grows out of the ground
- **HEAL**: to get better
  **HEEL**: the back part of the foot
- **HOLE**: an opening
  **WHOLE**: all of something
- **INSURE**: to have insurance (*I need to insure my car.*)
  **ENSURE**: to make sure something happens (*She ensured that the dog found a good home.*)
- **MEAT**: the flesh of an animal
  **MEET**: to see someone
- **MORNING**: the start of the day
  **MOURNING**: grieving
- **PATIENCE**: tolerating annoyances
  **PATIENTS**: people receiving medical care
- **PEACE**: not at war
  **PIECE**: a part of something
- **POOR**: having very little money
  **POUR**: to dispense from a container
- **PRINCIPAL**: the leader or administrative head of a school
  **PRINCIPLE**: a strongly held belief
- **RAIN**: precipitation
  **REIN**: a strap that controls an animal
  **REIGN**: to rule over
- **RIGHT**: correct; a legal entitlement
  **RITE**: a ritual
  **WRITE**: to put words on paper
- **STAIR**: used to get from one floor to another
  **STARE**: a long, fixed look
- **SUITE**: a set of rooms
  **SWEET**: the taste associated with sugar
- **THEIR**: belonging to them (*they brought their luggage*)
  **THERE**: a place (*the luggage is over there*)
  **THEY'RE**: they are (*they're looking for the luggage*)
- **THROUGH**: to go in one side and out the other
  **THREW**: tossed (past tense of *throw*)
- **TO**: the preposition indicating movement or purpose (*I am going to work to do my job.*)
  **TOO**: in addition (*I'm coming too.*)
  **TWO**: more than one; dual (*two officers patrol this area together*)
- **WEAR**: to put on (*I'll wear my new dress.*)
  **WHERE**: to question about place (*Where is the door?*)
- **YOUR**: belonging to you (*your car*)
  **YOU'RE**: you are (*you're going to need a new car*)

## Commonly Confused Words

Some words are similar in meaning, but not synonyms. However, they are commonly confused in writing and speech. A hallmark of good writing is the proper use of these words.

Table 2.8 contains some commonly confused words.

Table 2.8. Commonly Confused Words

| CONFUSED WORDS | DEFINITION |
| --- | --- |
| Amount | describes a noncountable quantity (*an unknown amount of jewelry was stolen*) |
| Number | describes a countable quantity (*an unknown number of necklaces was stolen*) |
| Bring | toward the speaker (*bring to me*) |
| Take | away from the speaker (*take away from me*) |
| Farther | a measurable distance (*the house farther up the road*) |
| Further | more or greater (*explain further what you mean*) |
| Fewer | a smaller amount of something plural (*fewer chairs*) |
| Less | a smaller amount of something that cannot be counted (*less water*) |
| Lose | to fail to win; to not be able to find something (*to lose a game; to lose one's keys*) |
| Loose | relaxed; not firmly in place (*my pants are loose*) |

## Special Spelling Rules

*i* comes before *e* except after *c*

Generally, the letter *i* comes before the letter *e* in a word except when the *i* is preceded by the letter *c*.

- p<u>ie</u>ce
- sal<u>ie</u>nt
- <u>cei</u>ling
- con<u>cei</u>vable

Be cautious of the rule "*i* comes before *e* except after *c*," for it has many exceptions: "Your foreign neighbors weighed the iciest beige glaciers!"

There are some notable exceptions where the letter e comes before the letter i, such as:

- words that end in *–cie*, like *proficient* or *ancient*
- plural words ending in *–cies*, like *policies*
- words with an *ay* sound, like *eight*, *vein*, or *neighbor*

When adding a suffix to a word, change the final *y* to an *i*.

- lazy → laziest
- tidy → tidily

For words that end with the letters *–le*, replace the letter *e* with the letter *y*: subtle → subtly

## Plurals

Regular nouns are made plural by adding *s*. Irregular nouns can follow many different rules for pluralization, which are summarized in the table below.

Table 2.9. Irregular Plural Nouns

| ENDS WITH... | MAKE IT PLURAL BY... | EXAMPLE |
| --- | --- | --- |
| y | changing *y* to *i* and adding *–es* | baby → babies |
| f | changing *f* to *v* and adding *–es* | leaf → leaves |
| fe | changing *f* to *v* and adding *–s* | knife → knives |
| o | adding *–es* | potato → potatoes |
| us | changing *–us* to *–i* | nucleus → nuclei |

| ALWAYS THE SAME | DOESN'T FOLLOW THE RULES |
| --- | --- |
| sheep | man → men |
| deer | child → children |
| fish | person → people |
| moose | tooth → teeth |
| pants | goose → geese |
| binoculars | mouse → mice |
| scissors | ox → oxen |

Pluralize words ending in *–ch, –s, –sh, –x,* or *–z* by adding *–es* to the end.

- catch → catches
- pass → passes
- push → pushes
- annex → annexes
- blitz → blitzes

An exception to the *–ch* rule includes words where the *ch* makes a *k* sound. For those words, simply add the letter *s* to the end of the word: stomach → stomachs.

## Possessives Versus Contractions

A **CONTRACTION** is a combination of two words that is shortened by using an apostrophe to indicate the missing letter or letters. For instance, *cannot* is shortened to *can't*; the apostrophe stands in for the missing letters *n* and *o*.

A **POSSESSIVE** is a word with an apostrophe added to indicate possession. For example, rather than writing "the duty belt that belongs to Pat," write "Pat's duty belt."

A notable exception to this rule—and a common mistake—is the improper use of the contraction *it's* as a possessive, *its*.

The contraction for *it is* or *it has* is *it's*: "It's dangerous in that area of town at night."

The word *its* is possessive and shows ownership of the pronoun *it*, such as "the jury reached *its* verdict" or "the suspect's car was badly damaged, and *its* license plate was obscured."

## Conjugating Verbs

The suffixes *–ed* or *–ing* added to a regular verb generally signify the verb's tense. For example, the present tense of the verb *to question* is *question* ("You question the suspect while I write the report.")

To show that the event happened in the past (or to form the past tense), the word *question* becomes *questioned*. And to refer to an action that is still happening (or to form the present participle), *question* becomes *questioning*. (See above for more details on conjugating verbs.)

There are some exceptions to the general rules for conjugating regular verbs.

For verbs ending with a silent *–e*, drop the *–e* before adding *–ed* or *–ing*.

- fake → faked → faking
- ache → ached → aching

When verbs end in the letters *–ee*, do not drop the second *e*. Instead, simply add *–d* or *–ing*.

- free → freed → freeing
- agree → agreed → agreeing

When the verb ends with a single vowel plus a consonant, and the stress is at the end of the word, then the consonant must be doubled before adding *–ed* or *–ing*.

- commit → committed → committing
- refer → referred → referring

If the stress is not at the end of the word, then the consonant can remain singular.

- target → targeted → targeting
- visit → visited → visiting

Verbs that end with the letter *c* must have the letter *k* added before receiving a suffix: panic → panicked → panicking

### Examples

*Read the following sentences and choose the correct spelling of the missing word.*

**21.** The defendant asked the court to show him _____ in the punishment for his crime.
- **(A)** lienency
- **(B)** leniency
- **(C)** leneincy
- **(D)** leanency

22. Deputy Smith found _____ in the inmate's cell.
    (A) contriband
    (B) controband
    (C) contraband
    (D) contreband

23. Evidence that is fleeting or that can fade away over time is said to be of an _____ nature.
    (A) effervescent
    (B) evanecent
    (C) evanescent
    (D) evenescent

24. Officer Jones attempted to _____ the victim's blood loss by applying pressure to the wound.
    (A) mitagate
    (B) mitegate
    (C) midigate
    (D) mitigate

# Answer Key

1. **(C) Correct.** *Minnesota* and *August* are proper nouns, and *coat* and *gloves* are common nouns. *I* is a pronoun, and *warm* is an adjective that modifies coat.

2. **(A) Correct.** *New* modifies the noun *chef*, and *boiling* modifies the noun *soup*.
   (B) Incorrect. *Carefully* is an adverb modifying the verb *stirred*.
   (C) Incorrect. *Heat* is a noun.
   (D) Incorrect. *Lowered* is a verb.

3. (A) Incorrect. *To* frequently indicates position; it does not make sense here.
   (B) Incorrect. *With* often implies a physical connection; it does not make sense here.
   **(C) Correct.** The correct preposition is *of*. The preposition *of* usually shows a relationship and may accompany a verb.
   (D) Incorrect. *About* is not idiomatically paired with *love* and is thus incorrect.

4. **(A) Correct.** Choice A should use quotation marks to set off a direct quote: *"I love apple pie!" John exclaimed with a smile.*

5. **(B) Correct.** The sentence is a question, so it should end with a question mark.

6. **(A) Correct.** The phrase is a prepositional phrase beginning with the preposition *with*. The preposition *with* modifies *the eager students*.

7. **(A) Correct.** In this sentence, the conjunction is joining together two contrasting ideas, so the correct answer is *but*.

8. (A) Incorrect. In this sentence, *hats* and *shoes* and *them* are all plural; they agree.
   **(B) Correct.** *The members of the band* is plural (*members*), so it should be replaced by the plural pronoun *their* instead of the singular *her*.
   (C) Incorrect. *Janitor* is singular, so the singular pronouns *his or her* are correct.
   (D) Incorrect. *You* and *you* agree in person and number. Note here that the pronoun *them* agrees with the antecedent *someone*. This is generally accepted usage, but it is unlikely to appear on an exam.

9. **(B) Correct.** Choice A contains a vague reference; it is unclear who was shot.

10. **(B) Correct.** This sentence contains a verb error; the verb *is* should be plural: *are*. All plural indefinite pronouns agree with plural verbs. Here, the subject of the sentence, *some*, is a plural indefinite pronoun, so it requires a plural verb.

11. **(A) Correct.** The phrase *by this time tomorrow* describes an action that will take place and be completed in the future, so the future perfect tense (*will have arrived*) should be used.

12. **(D) Correct.** This sentence should read, "Of the four speeches, Jerry's was the longest." The word *long* has only one syllable, so it should be modified with the suffix *–est*, not the word *most*.

13. **(A) Correct.** Choice B has a misplaced modifier (the word *often*).

14. **(A) Correct.** Choice B contains a sentence fragment.

15. **(B) Correct.** Choice A is a run-on sentence.

16. (A) Incorrect. *Inactive* means *dormant*.
    **(B) Correct.** *Unsettled* means *outstanding* or *due*.
    (C) Incorrect. *Unconfirmed* means *unsupported* or *uncorroborated*.
    (D) Incorrect. *Confirmed* means *verified*.

17. (A) Incorrect. *Confident* means *sure* or *secure*.
    (B) Incorrect. *Unsafe* means *dangerous* or *risky*.
    **(C) Correct.** *Self-satisfied* means *complacent*.
    (D) Incorrect. *Cheerful* means *pleasant* or *happy*.

18. (A) Incorrect. *Affirmed* means *to maintain as true* or *confirm*.
    **(B) Correct.** *Rescinded* means *recant*.
    (C) Incorrect. *Retold* means *told over again in a new way*.
    (D) Incorrect. *Regretted* means *felt remorse for*.

19. **(A) Correct.** *Trustworthy* means *credible*.
    (B) Incorrect. *Likeable* means *easy to like*.
    (C) Incorrect. *Suitable* means *appropriate*.
    (D) Incorrect. *Useful* means *being of use*.

20. (A) Incorrect. *Falsities* means *lies*.
    (B) Incorrect. *Inaccuracies* means *errors* or *mistakes*.
    (C) Incorrect. *Deception* means *ruse* or *trick*.
    **(D) Correct.** *Inconsistencies* means *discrepancies*.

21. **(B) Correct.** *Leniency* is the correct spelling.

22. **(C) Correct.** *Contraband* is the correct spelling.

23. **(C) Correct.** *Evanescent* is the correct spelling.

24. **(D) Correct.** *Mitigate* is the correct spelling.

# MATHEMATICS

## MATHEMATICAL OPERATIONS

The four basic arithmetic operations are addition, subtraction, multiplication, and division.

- **ADD** to combine two quantities (6 + 5 = 11).
- **SUBTRACT** to find the difference of two quantities (10 − 3 = 7).
- **MULTIPLY** to add a quantity multiple times (4 × 3 = 12).
- **DIVIDE** to find out how many times one quantity goes into another (10 ÷ 2 = 5).

On the exam, operations questions might be word problems. These problems will contain clue words that help you determine which operation to use.

Table 3.1. Operations Word Problems

| OPERATION | CLUE WORDS | EXAMPLE |
| --- | --- | --- |
| Addition | sum, (al)together, (in) total, all, in addition, increased, give | Officer Manley arrested 7 criminals yesterday and 3 today. How many did he arrest **altogether**? 7 + 3 = 10 criminals |
| Subtraction | minus, less than, take away, decreased, difference, How many left?, How many more/less? | The convicted felon was given 17 years in jail. His sentence was **reduced** by 5 years. How many years must he serve? 17 − 5 = 12 years |
| Multiplication | product, times, of, each/every, groups of, twice | **Each** magazine of a gun holds 20 bullets. How many bullets would 5 magazines hold? 20 × 5 = 100 bullets |
| Division | divided, per, each/every, distributed, average, How many for each?, How many groups? | There were 420 arrests made last year by 7 members of the police force. Assuming that **each** officer made the same number of arrests, **how many** arrests is that **per** officer? 420 ÷ 7 = 60 arrests per person |

### Examples

1. A typical police car carries 140 pounds of equipment. There are 7 cars at the station. How much total weight do the cars carry?

2. When working special events, police officers receive a bonus of $50 plus $30 for each hour worked. How much would an officer receive if she worked a concert for 4 hours?

## OPERATIONS WITH POSITIVE AND NEGATIVE NUMBERS

Positive numbers are greater than zero, and negative numbers are less than zero. Use the rules in Table 3.2 to determine the sign of the answer when performing operations with positive and negative numbers.

Table 3.2. Operations with Positive and Negative Numbers

| ADDITION AND SUBTRACTION | MULTIPLICATION AND DIVISION |
|---|---|
| positive + positive = positive<br>4 + 5 = 9 | positive × positive = positive<br>5 × 3 = 15 |
| negative + negative = negative<br>−4 + −5 = −9 → −4 − 5 = −9 | negative × negative = positive<br>−6 × −5 = 30 |
| negative + positive = sign of the larger number<br>−15 + 9 = −6 | negative × positive = negative<br>−5 × 4 = −20 |

> ⚠ Subtracting a negative number is the same as adding a positive number:
> 5 − (−10) = 5 + (+10) = 5 + 10 = 15

A **NUMBER LINE** shows numbers increasing from left to right (usually with zero in the middle). When adding positive and negative numbers, a number line can be used to find the sign of the answer. When adding a positive number, count to the right; when adding a negative number, count to the left. Note that adding a negative value is the same as subtracting.

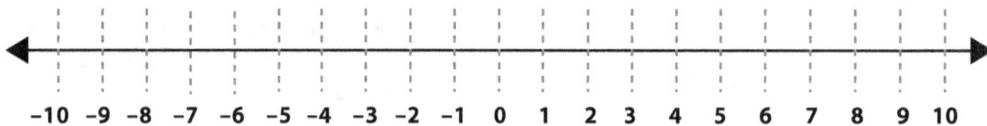

Figure 3.1. Adding Positive and Negative Numbers

### Example

3. The wind chill on a cold day in January was −3°F. When the sun went down, the temperature fell 5 degrees. What was the temperature after the sun went down?

## FRACTIONS

A **FRACTION** represents parts of a whole. The top number of a fraction, called the **NUMERATOR**, indicates how many equal-sized parts are present. The bottom number of a fraction, called the **DENOMINATOR**, indicates how many equal-sized parts make a whole.

Fractions have several forms:

- **PROPER FRACTION**: the numerator is less than the denominator
- **IMPROPER FRACTION**: the numerator is greater than or equal to the denominator
- **MIXED NUMBER**: the combination of a whole number and a fraction

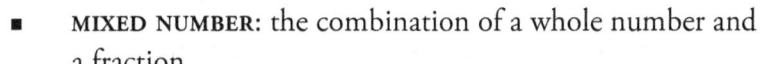

*Figure 3.2. Parts of Fractions*

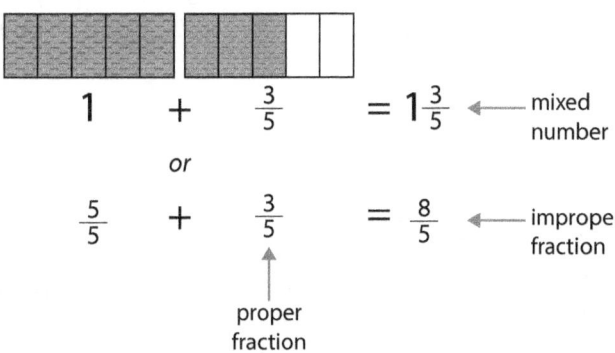

*Figure 3.3. Types of Fractions*

Improper fractions can be converted to mixed numbers by dividing. In fact, the fraction bar is also a division symbol.

$$\frac{14}{3} = 14 \div 3 = 4 \text{ (with 2 left over)}$$
$$\frac{14}{3} = 4\frac{2}{3}$$

To convert a mixed number to a fraction, multiply the whole number by the denominator of the fraction, and add the numerator. The result becomes the numerator of the improper fraction; the denominator remains the same.

$$5\frac{2}{3} = \frac{(5 \times 3) + 2}{3} = \frac{17}{3}$$

To **MULTIPLY FRACTIONS**, multiply numerators and multiply denominators. Reduce the product to lowest terms. To **DIVIDE FRACTIONS**, multiply the dividend (the first fraction) by the reciprocal of the divisor (the fraction that follows the division symbol).

When multiplying and dividing mixed numbers, the mixed numbers must be converted to improper fractions.

Adding or subtracting fractions requires a common denominator. To find a **COMMON DENOMINATOR**, multiply the denominators of the fractions. Then, to add the fractions, add the numerators and keep the denominator the same.

> ⚠ The reciprocal of a fraction is just the fraction with the top and bottom numbers switched.

**Examples**

4. $7\frac{1}{2} \times 1\frac{5}{6} =$

**MATHEMATICS** 41

5. Officer Williams completed $\frac{1}{4}$ of the paperwork for the week, and Officer Thompson completed $\frac{1}{3}$ of the paperwork for the week. What fraction of the work did they complete together?

# DECIMALS

In the base-10 system, each digit (the numeric symbols 0 – 9) in a number is worth ten times as much as the number to the right of it. For example, in the number 321 each digit has a different value based on its location: 321 = 300 + 20 + 1. The value of each place is called **PLACE VALUE**.

Table 3.3. Place Value Chart

| 1,000,000 | 100,000 | 10,000 | 1,000 | 100 | 10 | 1 | | $\frac{1}{10}$ | $\frac{1}{100}$ |
|---|---|---|---|---|---|---|---|---|---|
| $10^6$ | $10^5$ | $10^4$ | $10^3$ | $10^2$ | $10^1$ | $10^0$ | . | $10^{-1}$ | $10^{-2}$ |
| millions | hundred thousands | ten thousands | thousands | hundreds | tens | ones | decimal | tenths | hundredths |

To **ADD DECIMAL NUMBERS**, line up digits with the same place value. This can be accomplished by writing the numbers vertically and lining up the decimal points. Add zeros as needed so that all the numbers have the same number of decimal places.

To **SUBTRACT DECIMAL NUMBERS**, follow the same procedure: write the numbers vertically, lining up the decimal points and adding zeros as necessary.

It is not necessary to line up decimal points to **MULTIPLY DECIMAL NUMBERS**. Simply multiply the numbers, ignoring the decimal point. Then, add together the total number of decimal places in the factors. The product should have the same number of decimal places as this total.

To **DIVIDE DECIMAL NUMBERS**, write the problem in long division format. Move the decimal point in the divisor all the way to the right, so that the divisor is a whole number. Move the decimal point in the dividend the same number of places. Position the decimal point in the quotient directly above its new place in the dividend. Then divide, ignoring the decimal point. If necessary, add zeros to the dividend until there is no remainder.

*Figure 3.4. Division Terms*

### Examples

6. At the Starlight Diner, Officer Jenkins ordered a drink that cost $2.20, a meal that cost $32.54, and a dessert that cost $4. How much was the total bill?

7. When walking through the neighborhood on patrol, a typical police officer covers 3.2 miles per hour. If she walked for 4.5 hours, how many miles of the neighborhood did she patrol?

8. 1.324 ÷ 0.05 =

# RATIOS

A **RATIO** is a comparison of two quantities. For example, if a class consists of fifteen women and ten men, the ratio of women to men is 15 to 10. This ratio can also be written as 15:10 or $\frac{15}{10}$. Ratios, like fractions, can be reduced by dividing by common factors.

### Example

9. Thirty officers and staff members work at a local precinct, 12 of whom are men. What is the ratio of women to men working at the precinct?

# PROPORTIONS

A **PROPORTION** is a statement that two ratios are equal. For example, proportion $\frac{5}{10} = \frac{7}{14}$ is true because both ratios are equal to $\frac{1}{2}$.

The cross product is found by multiplying the top of one fraction by the bottom of the other (across the equal sign).

$$\text{Cross product: } \frac{a}{b} = \frac{c}{d} \rightarrow ad = bc$$

Proportions have a useful quality: their cross products are equal.

$$\frac{5}{10} = \frac{7}{14}$$
$$5(14) = 7(10)$$
$$70 = 70$$

The fact that the cross products of proportions are equal can be used to solve proportions in which one of the values is missing. Use *x* to stand in for the missing variable, then cross multiply and solve.

### Example

10. An event organizer would like to have 5 officers for every 700 people at an event. If the event is going to have 2000 people, about how many officers should be at the event?

# PERCENTAGES

A **PERCENTAGE** (or percent) means *per hundred* and is expressed with the percent symbol, %. For example, 54% means 54 out of every 100. Percentages are turned into decimals by moving the decimal point two places to the left, so 54% = 0.54. Percentages can be solved by setting up a proportion:

$$\frac{\text{part}}{\text{whole}} = \frac{\%}{100}$$

### Example

11. At a police safety belt checkpoint, 5% of the people were not correctly wearing their seat belt. If 500 drivers came through the checkpoint, how many people were not correctly wearing their seatbelt?

# Estimation and Rounding

Estimation is the process of rounding numbers before performing operations in order to make those operations easier. Estimation can be used when an exact answer is not necessary or to check work.

To round a number, first identify the digit in the specified place. Then look at the digit one place to the right. If that digit is 4 or less, keep the digit in the specified place the same. If that digit is 5 or more, add 1 to the digit in the specified place. All the digits to the right of the specified place become zeros.

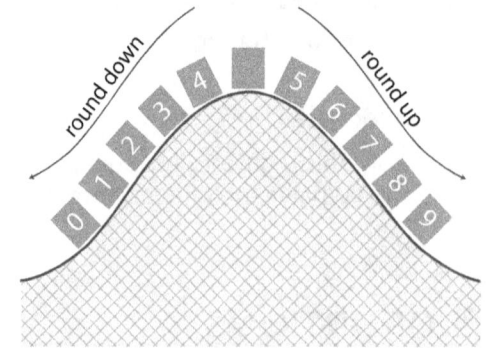

*Figure 3.5. Rounding*

**Example**

12. The cost of a police shirt is $45.75, and the cost of pants is $32.30. Estimate the total cost of these 2 items.

# Units

The United States uses *customary units*, sometimes called *standard units*. In this system, there are a number of different units that can be used to describe the same variable. These units and the relationships between them are shown in Table 3.4.

Table 3.4. US Customary Units

| VARIABLE MEASURED | UNIT | CONVERSIONS |
| --- | --- | --- |
| Length | inches, foot, yard, mile | 12 inches = 1 foot<br>3 feet = 1 yard<br>5,280 feet = 1 mile |
| Weight | ounces, pound, ton | 16 ounces = 1 pound<br>2,000 pounds = 1 ton |
| Volume | fluid ounces, cup, pint, quart, gallon | 8 fluid ounces = 1 cup<br>2 cups = 1 pint<br>2 pints = 1 quart<br>4 quarts = 1 gallon |
| Time | second, minute, hour, day | 60 seconds = 1 minute<br>60 minutes = 1 hour<br>24 hours = 1 day |
| Area | square inch, square food, square yard | 144 square inches = 1 square foot<br>9 square feet = 1 square yard |

Most other countries use the metric system, which has its own set of units for variables like length, weight, and volume. These units are modified by prefixes that make large and small numbers easier to handle. These units and prefixes are shown in Table 3.5.

Table 3.5. Metric Units and Prefixes

| VARIABLE MEASURED | BASE UNIT |
|---|---|
| length | meter |
| weight | gram |
| volume | liter |

| METRIC PREFIX | CONVERSION |
|---|---|
| kilo | base unit × 1,000 |
| hecto | base unit × 100 |
| deka | base unit × 10 |
| deci | base unit × 0.1 |
| centi | base unit × 0.01 |
| milli | base unit × 0.001 |

**CONVERSION FACTORS** are used to convert one unit to another (either within the same system or between different systems). A conversion factor is simply a fraction built from two equivalent values. For example, there are 12 inches in 1 foot, so the conversion factor can be $\frac{12 \text{ in.}}{1 \text{ ft.}}$ or $\frac{1 \text{ ft.}}{12 \text{ in.}}$.

To convert from one unit to another, multiple the original value by a conversion factor that has the old and new units.

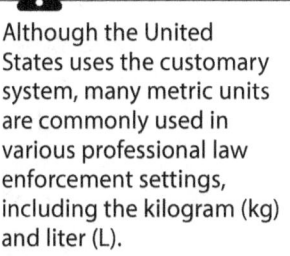

Although the United States uses the customary system, many metric units are commonly used in various professional law enforcement settings, including the kilogram (kg) and liter (L).

How many inches are in 6 feet?

$$6 \text{ ft.} \times \frac{12 \text{ in.}}{1 \text{ ft.}} = \frac{6 \text{ ft.} \times 12 \text{ in.}}{1 \text{ ft.}} = 72 \text{ in.}$$

**Examples**

13. How many centimeters are in 2.5 m?

14. A police officer should consume 30 ounces of water per hour when working in the sun. If Officer Jones worked 6 hours in the sun, how many pints of water should he drink?

## PERIMETER AND AREA

**PERIMETER** is the distance around a shape. It can be found by adding the lengths of all the shape's sides. **AREA** is the amount of space a shape occupies. The area of an object is its length times its width and is measured in square units. For example, if a wall is 3 feet long and 2 feet wide, its area would be 6 square feet (ft²).

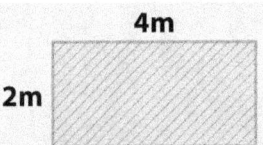

Perimeter = the sum of all sides = 2 m + 4 m + 2 m + 4 m = 12 m

Area = the length times the width = 2 m × 4 m = 8 m²

**MATHEMATICS**

Table 3.6 gives the formulas for the area and perimeter of basic shapes. To find the area and perimeter of a circle, use the constant pi ($\pi = 3.14$).

Table 3.6. Area and Perimeter of Basic Shapes

| SHAPE | | AREA | PERIMETER |
|---|---|---|---|
| Triangle | | $A = \frac{1}{2}bh$ | $P = s_1 + s_2 + s_3$ |
| Square | | $A = s^2$ | $P = 4s$ |
| Rectangle | | $A = l \times w$ | $P = 2l + 2w$ |
| Circle | | $A = \pi r^2$ | $C = 2\pi r$ (Circumference) |

## Examples

15. The polygon below is regular, which means each of its side is the same length. What is its perimeter?

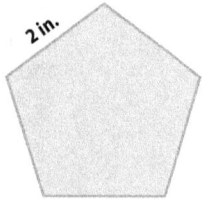

16. What is the area of the shape below?

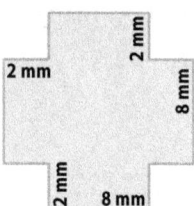

# ANSWER KEY

1. Multiply the total weight of 1 car by the total number of cars.

   140 × 7 = **980 pounds**

2. The officer's bonus is $50 plus an additional $30 per hour.

   4(30) + 50 =

   120 + 50 = **$170**

3. Because the temperature went down, add a negative number.

   −3 + −5 = **−8°F**

4. Convert the mixed numbers to improper fractions.

   $7\frac{1}{2} = \frac{7 \times 2 + 1}{2} = \frac{15}{2}$

   $1\frac{5}{6} = \frac{1 \times 6 + 5}{6} = \frac{11}{6}$

   Multiply the numerators, multiply the denominators, and reduce.

   $\frac{15}{2} \times \frac{11}{6} = \frac{165}{12} = \frac{165 \div 3}{12 \div 3} = \frac{55}{4}$

5. The common denominator is 4 × 3 = 12.

   Convert each fraction to the common denominator.

   $\frac{1}{4}(\frac{3}{3}) = \frac{3}{12}$

   $\frac{1}{3}(\frac{4}{4}) = \frac{4}{12}$

   Add the numerators and keep the denominator the same.

   $\frac{3}{12} + \frac{4}{12} = \frac{7}{12}$

   **Together, they have done $\frac{7}{12}$ of the work.**

6. Rewrite the numbers vertically, lining up the decimal point.

   2.20
   32.54
   + 4.00
   38.74

   The meal cost **$38.74**.

7. This is a multiplication problem. Use the formula rate × time = distance.

   3.2 mph × 4.5 hrs. = **14.4 total miles**

8. The decimal point in the divisor needs to be moved two places to the right, so move it two places to the right in the divisor as well. Then position the decimal point in the quotient.

   ```
         26.48
   005 ) 132.40
         −10
          32
         −30
          24
         −20
          40
         −40
           0
   ```

9. Find the number of women working at the precinct.

   30 − 12 = 18 women

   Write the ratio as the number of women over the number of men working at the precinct.

   $\frac{\text{number of women}}{\text{number of men}} = \frac{18}{12}$

   Reduce the ratio.

   $\frac{18 \div 6}{12 \div 6} = \frac{3}{2}$

   **The ratio of women to men is $\frac{3}{2}$ or 3:2.**

MATHEMATICS

10.

| | |
|---|---|
| $\frac{5}{700} = \frac{x}{2000}$ | Write a proportion for the missing value. |
| $700(x) = 5(2000)$ | Cross multiply. |
| $700x = 10,000$ | Divide by 700. |
| $x = 14.29$ $x \approx 14$ | Solve. |

**The answer is about 14 officers.**

11. Multiply 5% × 500.

    0.05 × 500 = 25, so **25 people were not correctly wearing their seatbelt**.

12. Solve the problem by rounding the expenses to the nearest $10.

    $45.75 rounds up to $50 because the digit in the ones place is 5.

    $32.30 rounds down to $30 because the digit in the ones place is 2.

    50 + 30 = 80, so **the total cost is about $80**.

13. Use a conversion factor to convert centimeters to meters.

    $2.5 \text{ m} \times \frac{100 \text{ cm}}{1 \text{ m}} = \frac{2.5 \text{ m} \times 100 \text{ cm}}{1 \text{ m}} =$ **250 cm**

14. Find the total number of ounces that he should drink.

    30 × 6 = 180 ounces

    Use a conversion factor to convert ounces to pints.

    $180 \text{ oz.} \times \frac{1 \text{ cup}}{8 \text{ oz.}} \times \frac{1 \text{ pt.}}{2 \text{ cups}} =$ **11.25 pints**

15. Add the lengths of the sides to find the perimeter:

    2 in. + 2 in. + 2 in. + 2 in. + 2 in. = **10 in.**

16. Break the shape into squares and rectangles, and then find the area of each smaller shape.

    The area of each rectangle is $A = l \times w$.

    $A = 8 \text{ mm} \times 2 \text{ mm} = 16 \text{ mm}^2$

    The area of the center square is $A = s^2$.

    $A = 8 \text{ mm} \times 8 \text{ mm} = 64 \text{ mm}^2$

    Add the four rectangles and the center square:

    $4(16 \text{ mm}^2) + 64 \text{ mm}^2 =$ **128 mm²**

# REASONING FOR LAW ENFORCEMENT

## WHAT IS REASONING?

**REASONING** is the ability to apply logical skills and cognitive aptitudes to the **FACTS** (i.e., the indisputable evidence or crucial pieces of information) of a situation in order to make a sound decision. Officers use **LOGIC** to assess and organize the facts or evidence of a particular scenario or situation. Reasoning is tested in the field of criminal justice because police officers, state troopers, and correctional officers work under life-and-death circumstances that demand they acutely understand complex relationships and convey a clear understanding of the most important facts.

## INDUCTIVE REASONING

### What is Inductive Reasoning?

Within the context of law enforcement or corrections, inductive reasoning is the ability to analyze the facts in order to hypothesize whether a particular rule, trend, or concept fits the situation or scenario. This analytical skill comes in handy when trying to understand the events or sequence of a particular crime or trying to trace/map a series of related crimes. It also comes in handy when analyzing any kind of chart, graph, or data.

### How is Inductive Reasoning Tested in Law Enforcement?

In law enforcement certification examinations, test takers must draw conclusions about quantitative information provided in the form of charts, graphs, or data sets. They must deduce which rules, trends, or concepts fit the quantitative information offered.

    **CHARTS** are data visualization tools that outline or exhibit certain data sets or categories, usually in tabular form. **TABLES**, which might look like an Excel spreadsheet, list key facts and compare these facts across categories via rows and columns. The top row, as illustrated in the table in Figure 4.1, is usually the *title row* with all the titles of each column. The first column usually dictates the main category (in Figure 4.1, "Year/degree of injury") that will be compared across the other column categories. The other column categories in this table include "Fatal," Serious," "Slight," and "Total." In this particular table, there are computations offered in the last column ("Total") and the last row ("Percent increase"). All rows offer the concrete numerical data that ties the dates of the first column with the categories of the top row.

| YEAR/DEGREE OF INJURY | FATAL | SERIOUS | SLIGHT | TOTAL |
|---|---|---|---|---|
| 1998 – 1999 | 49 | 162 | 653 | **864** |
| 1999 – 2000 | 62 | 200 | 933 | **1195** |
| 2000 – 2001 | 72 | 244 | 1066 | **1382** |
| 2001 – 2002 | 95 | 392 | 1390 | **1877** |
| 2002 – 2003 | 80 | 416 | 1683 | **2179** |
| 2003 – 2004 | 68 | 437 | 1862 | **2367** |
| 2004 – 2005 | 77 | 411 | 3424 | **3912** |
| 2005 – 2006 | 49 | 476 | 3296 | **3821** |
| 2006 – 2007 | 58 | - | - | - |
| Percent increase 98/99–05/06 or 06/07 | 18 | 194 | 405 | **342** |

*Figure 4.1. Table*

A **GRAPH** is a data visualization diagram that represents that variation of a variable in comparison to one or more differing variables. All graphs have labels.

- The **MAIN TITLE** offers a brief explanation of what is in the graph. Titles help the audience to understand the "main point" or "main claim" of a graph.
- The **SUBTITLE** offers more specific information about the purpose of the graph. Subtitles are brief sentences or phrases that enhance main titles.
- Bar graphs and line graphs have an *X*-**AXIS**; the *x*-axis runs horizontally (flat). The *x*-axis has quantities representing different categories, statistics, or times that are being compared.
- Bar graphs and line graphs have a *Y*-**AXIS**; the *y*-axis runs vertically (up and down). The *y*-axis usually measures quantities, typically starting at 0 or another designated number.

The two generic graphs in Figures 4.2 and 4.3—a bar graph and a line graph—illustrate where labels are located. In some cases, the subtitle can be placed below or beside the main title.

Both types of graphs—bar graphs and line graphs—show *trends*, or prevailing developments, tendencies, or inclinations that can be extrapolated from the graph. The trends of the **BAR GRAPH** in Figure 4.2 compare two categories: male versus female (in terms of the broader category of victims of violent crime). **LINE GRAPHS**, on the other hand, usually show change over time. The trend that emerges in the bar graph is that, from 2013 to 2016, women were more likely to be the victims of violent crime. One trend that emerges in the line graph is that burglary declined from 2004 to 2008.

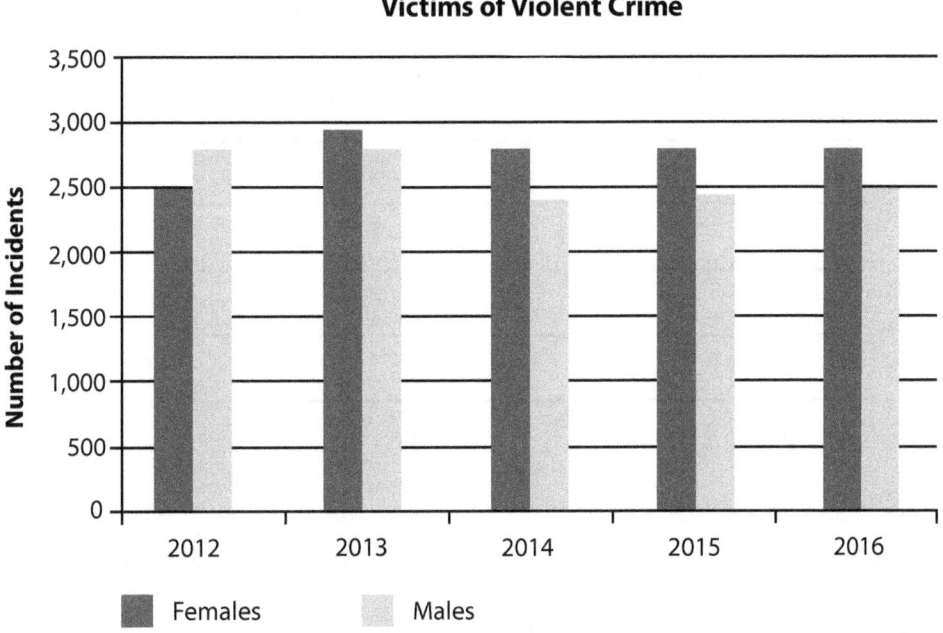

Figure 4.2. Bar Graph

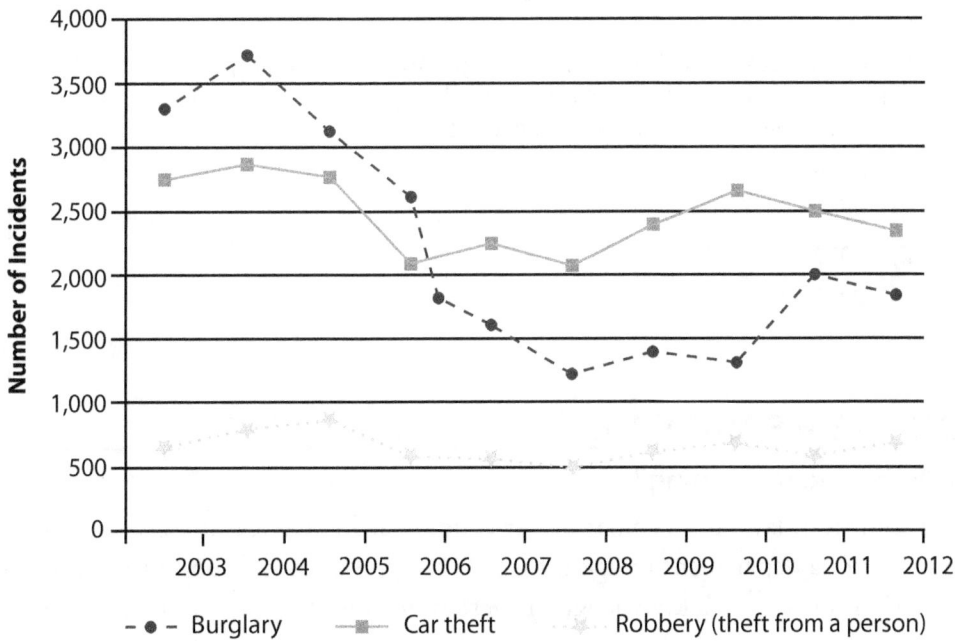

Figure 4.3. Line Graph

### Examples

*Use the graph to answer the questions below.*

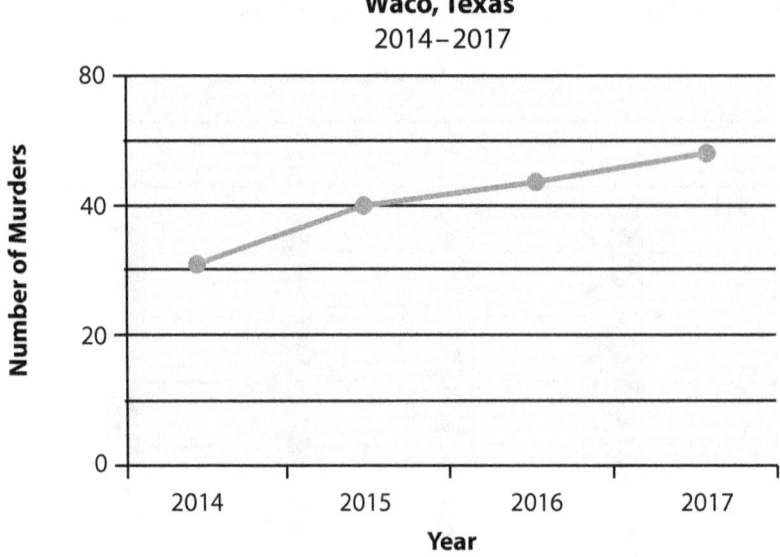

1. According to the graph above, what can be concluded about the murder rate in Waco, TX?
   A) It has declined from 2014 – 2017.
   B) It has increased from 2014 – 2017.
   C) It remained the same from 2014 – 2017.
   D) It increased in 2014 – 2016, but it decreased in 2017.

2. A program was recently instituted to fight against the rising murder rate in Waco, Texas. However, the program only lasted one year due to budget cuts. What year was this program most likely cut?
   A) 2014
   B) 2015
   C) 2016
   D) 2017

## DEDUCTIVE REASONING

### What is Deductive Reasoning?

Within the context of law enforcement or corrections, deductive reasoning is employed when a member of a department or agency is able to apply protocols and procedures to specific situations or use one's knowledge of these protocols and procedures to come to logical conclusions. One example of deductive reasoning is deciding whether to arrest an alleged perpetrator of a domestic incident based on the rules and regulations (i.e., the step-by-step details) provided by the department or agency. Deductive reasoning is useful in law enforcement or corrections because officers and agents are continually placed into situations where they must be able to apply the rules in order to reach a conclusion.

## How is Deductive Reasoning Tested in Law Enforcement?

On public safety certification exams, police officers and correctional officers must read passages that explain particular state or local policies. In order to demonstrate their deductive reasoning skills, they also have to read specific scenarios and decide the best course of action for approaching these scenarios based on the policies they just read.

### Examples

*Below is an example of a general domestic incident response order that may be used in a police department:*

#### I. POLICY

Domestic violence is a serious crime, one that affects both the individual and society. Our department seeks to reduce all incidents of domestic violence through coordinated partnerships with law enforcement agencies, victims, and communities. Recognizing that domestic violence escalates in its severity and frequency over time, our department advocates for early intervention, especially in households that have already been documented "at risk." Officers will treat these incidents in the same professional manner as all other law enforcement requests, providing immediate and effective assistance. Recognizing our state's Domestic Violence Act (DVA), we plan to protect victims from these devastating incidents, using all reasonable means necessary to prevent further abuse. These reasonable means may include the arrest of an alleged offender if there is probable cause.

#### II. INITIAL RESPONSE

I. Whenever a law enforcement officer responds to a domestic incident, he or she must immediately use all reasonable means to prevent further abuse, neglect, or exploitation. These means include the potential need to

1. restore order by asserting control of the situation.
2. identify and secure any weapons or objects that can be used as weapons.
3. determine if medical assistance is needed.
    a. If medical assistance is needed, the law enforcement officer must call for an ambulance or arrange for the victim's transfer to a hospital.
    b. If the victim refuses treatment, the law enforcement officer must advise the victim of the importance of getting medical attention.

II. If another department member is involved in the domestic incident, the responding member must request that a department member of higher rank be present.

*Answer the following questions using the information from the text.*

3. An officer arrives on scene at a domestic incident at 345 N. Landover Street. When the officer arrives at the residence, she realizes that the alleged perpetrator happens to be one of her fellow officers at the Landover Precinct. The fellow officer is wielding a weapon at his wife, who appears to be seriously injured. What is the proper sequence for responding to this situation, keeping in mind the general orders regarding domestic violence for the department?

    A) restore order by securing the weapon and the neutralizing the aggressor, call for an ambulance, notify a higher-ranking officer

    B) notify a higher-ranking officer, wait for the higher-ranking officer to arrive, and call for an ambulance

    C) call for an ambulance, notify a higher-ranking officer, and restore order by securing the weapon and the neutralizing the aggressor

    D) restore order by securing the weapon and the neutralizing the aggressor, call for an ambulance, and file the necessary paperwork

4. What happens if the victim refuses medical attention?

    A) take her into the precinct for private questioning

    B) respect her rights as a victim and simply document it in your paperwork

    C) advise the victim of the importance of getting medical attention

    D) report the incident to a higher-ranking police officer

# Problem Sensitivity

**Problem sensitivity** is the ability to use common sense to recognize that something is wrong or is likely to go wrong. Common sense is the ability to use common or basic facts (e.g., body language, evidence, or statements) to remain sensitive that there is or may be a problem. It is the ability to recognize that there is a problem embedded within a particular moment or situation. Police officers and correctional officers are expected to be sensitive to the *whole problem* as well as *the underlying components of that problem*. Using the ongoing example of domestic incidents, problem sensitivity would manifest itself in a law enforcement officer's ability to use signs (e.g., body language, evidence, or statements) to recognize that an underlying conflict might be in progress between family members.

On public safety certifications, problem sensitivity questions typically take form as a short passage that the test taker must read in order to extrapolate any major issues or problems. In some cases, the test taker may be asked to explain the conditions or root causes of the problem.

### Identifying, Not Solving, Problems

**Problem sensitivity** is not about being solution oriented. It is about paying extreme attention to detail, or having the ability to focus on specific components of a passage—in this case, to identify the problem or its root causes/conditions. It is also the ability to draw conclusions, or logically "pull information" (i.e., key words, facts, and sentences), from a text in order to make a claim. In this context, the claim is identifying the problem or its root causes/conditions.

You are not being tested on solving the problem. Rather, the exam is testing candidates on their ability to identify the problem and/or its root causes or conditions. The problem sensitivity portion of the exams is about paying attention to details and drawing conclusions that identify the problem(s) embedded in these details.

Below are examples of problem sensitivity questions you might see on an exam.

### Examples

Officers Morales and Davidson were called to the scene of an apparent physical altercation between a father and his eight-year-old son. The child had previously called 9-1-1, claiming that his father had punched him in the throat. Officer Morales approached the family to see if everything was all right. The child, now holding his father's hand, tells the officers in a wheezing voice that he was just lying because he was upset that his father took away his video games. He apologizes to the officers, claiming "all of this was my fault, I swear." Officer Davidson notices evident bruising along the child's neck as well as the apparent wheezing in his voice. Officer Morales also notices the father gripping the child's hand tightly. Officer Davidson asks the child why he has bruises and why he is wheezing. The boy anxiously replies that he had slipped and fell while he was throwing a fit over his video game. Both officers are suspicious of this story.

**5.** After analyzing this scenario, what important details can be extracted to use as evidence of a potential problem?
   **A)** the boy's statement that it was his fault
   **B)** the fact that the father and son were holding hands
   **C)** the boy's claim that it was about a dispute over video games
   **D)** the evident wheezing and bruising

Officer Bridges is patrolling a city park around 2:15 a.m. when he notices a car speeding through a stop sign on the closest street. He pulls the car over for a routine traffic stop. As he walks over to the vehicle, he notices the driver snap back quickly into a normal sitting position after fiddling around in the glove compartment. The driver remains stiff in posture, rapidly claiming, "I know I rolled that stop sign officer, but I am just a little tired." The driver says it "won't happen again" and asks for forgiveness just this one time. There are no signs of alcohol or drug use. The driver is cognizant but anxious. Officer Bridges asks the driver, "What were you doing in your glove compartment?" The driver snaps back: "What is it with you cops always being up in my business? Can't you just let me go? I just rolled a stop sign." The driver apologizes for "losing his cool," but ignores the initial question. When asked the question again, he ignores it and focuses back on the apology. A third attempt at the question has the same result for Officer Bridges.

**6.** Based on the details provided about the situation, what is likely the problem?
   A) The driver is just impatient and has little faith in police officers.
   B) The driver is intoxicated.
   C) The driver is concealing something in his glove compartment.
   D) The driver is hiding drugs in his glove compartment.

# SPATIAL ORIENTATION

### What is Spatial Orientation?

SPATIAL ORIENTATION questions attempt to assess the visualization ability of law enforcement officers. In particular, spatial orientation questions evaluate law enforcement or correctional officers' ability to understand their relation to a particular object, location, or set of objects or locations. Most certification exams provide test takers with a map (with a key and compass). The map is accompanied by a scenario. Typically, test takers have to use the map and the scenario to determine the shortest distance between locations or objects on the map. Likewise, spatial orientation questions may also quiz aspiring officers on the relationship(s) between objects and locations.

### Spatial Orientation in Law Enforcement

Spatial orientation requires both memorization (of place) and directional orientation. These skills are important for officers because they allow them to stay oriented once directions or locations are changed. Officers must be able to find quick routes to and from emergencies, and they must be able to change directions to effectively respond to crimes and/or crises.

### Examples

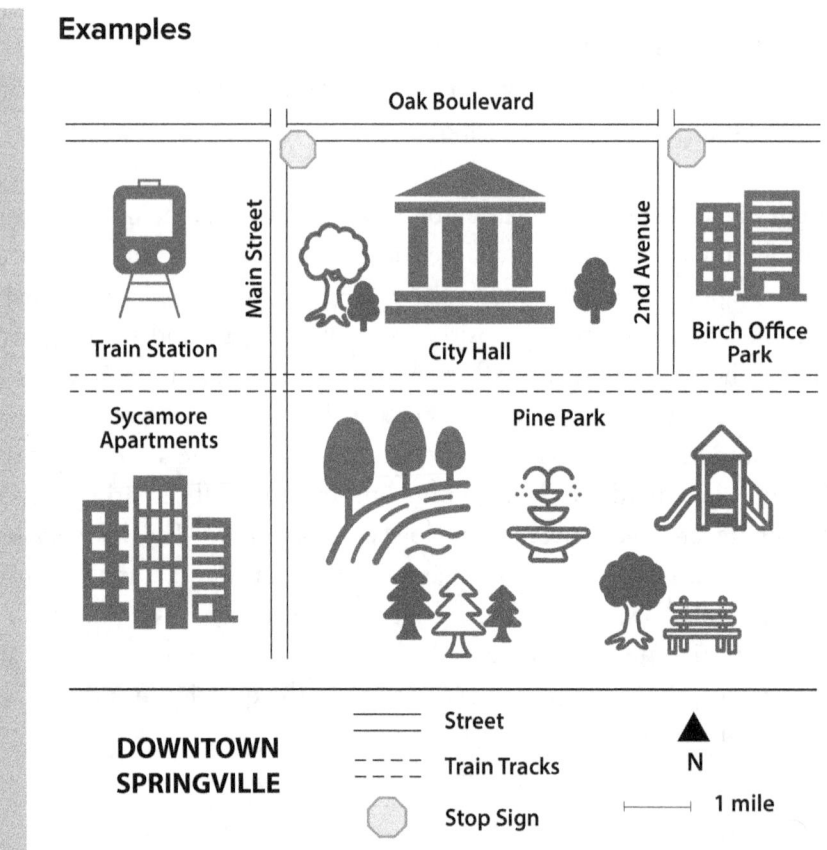

7. Officers Dalton and Mills have parked their police cruiser at the intersection of Second Avenue and the train tracks. They receive a call to respond to a violent assault at the southwestern corner of Pine Park. What is the only route they can take in their police cruiser to make it to the site of the incident?

   A) travel south on Second Avenue, west on Oak Boulevard, and north on Main Street
   B) travel north on Second Avenue, west on Oak Boulevard, and south on Main Street
   C) travel north on Second Avenue, east on Oak Boulevard, and north on Main Street
   D) travel north on Second Avenue, east on Oak Boulevard, and south on Main Street

8. A call from a concerned citizen at the Sycamore Apartments reported that she had witnessed a burglary from her window. The person claimed the burglary took place right on the street near Pine Park. Based on the map, the witness's window was likely facing

   A) north.
   B) south.
   C) east.
   D) west.

# Information Ordering

**Information ordering** is the power to apply the proper instructions, rules, or orders to a particular situation or scenario while maintaining an appropriate sequence. Information ordering assesses a candidate's ability to understand and apply procedures. This is important in law enforcement because many protocols, orders, and laws are sequential and procedural.

### Example
*Officer Lopez just finished responding to a domestic incident at 225 Main Street. The following seven statements appeared in the victim's recorded testimony:*

1. I ran upstairs to the bedroom to get away from the incident.
2. I locked the bedroom door behind me to prevent him from hitting me.
3. My husband got mad at me because I was denying the incident.
4. My husband claimed that I cheated on him with a neighbor.
5. I told him I was not a woman who would cheat on her husband.
6. He became so angry that he punched me in my jaw.
7. He kicked down the bedroom door, and that is when I called the police.

9. What is the most logical ordering of these statements?

   A) 1, 2, 3, 4, 5, 6, 7
   B) 2, 4, 3, 1, 6, 5, 7
   C) 4, 5, 3, 6, 1, 2, 7
   D) 1, 7, 4, 5, 3, 6, 2

# Memorization

**Memorization** is the ability to recall specific evidence, facts, or details about a certain policy, event, or incident. Memorization is a key skill for law enforcement and correctional officers because while on active duty, all officers need to observe and remember the details of an event or its contexts, and they need to be alert at every scene. Memorization is the foundation of observation and alertness in the field.

Observation and alertness allow officers to not only respond appropriately to dangerous situations, but also *recall* those situations for documentation, criminalization, and legal cases. Observation and alertness protect officers both on and off duty.

On criminal justice certification examinations, memorization questions usually follow the exhibition of a particular photograph (which is viewed for a limited amount of time). Aspiring officers have to recall what they witnessed in the photograph.

**Examples**

10. How many officers are depicted in the photograph?
    A) 1
    B) 2
    C) 3
    D) 4

11. Where was the picture most likely taken?
    A) by the railroad tracks
    B) at the police station
    C) on the side of the road
    D) in a parking lot

# VISUALIZATION

**VISUALIZATION** is the ability to conceptualize potential movements, additions, rearrangements, or reductions of a particular object or scene. Visualization questions in law enforcement evaluate how aspiring officers can form mental images of potential patterns. Mental images are best described as conceptual maps and images produced within the mind of an individual in order to recognize patterns or carry out a particular task. **RECONSTRUCTION**, which literally means "the process of constructing something again," is the ability to take these mental images and retell/reenact them. Reconstruction is a term used in law enforcement to describe the act of reimagining or reinventing a crime scene. This skill comes in handy when conjuring crime scene reconstructions or evaluating weapons for alterations. It also comes in handy when trying to recognize or fathom the potential appearance changes of suspects. Finally, visualization can assist an officer with searching scenes of alleged illicit activity; it can help officers produce the cognitive maps they need to carry out investigations.

### Example

*The large figure on the left can only be made from three of the four pieces to the right of it. Identify the letter of the piece that is NOT used.*

12.

# SELECTIVE ATTENTION

**SELECTIVE ATTENTION** is the ability to concentrate or remain on task when influenced by a constant stream of external stimuli or distractors. Selective attention questions evaluate an aspiring officer's ability to apply these skills. When on duty, law enforcement and correctional officers are bombarded daily with external stimuli or distractors, such as radio usage and other commotions, and they still have to focus on the **DETAILS** (specific facts, items, or features evident within an object or a scene). In most instances, these officers have to multitask while also being bombarded with numerous logistics. They may have to file paperwork or recall a license plate number while also listening to chatter on their dispatch radios.

Selective attention is important for officers because the need to maintain extreme focus in the midst of all this "noise." This focus is important for responding to emergencies and documenting incidents.

**Example**

13. Choose the option that contains the EXACT pattern of symbols, letters, numbers, and spaces.

    TUB5ScQ &=\\ /35Z!!!hE?ÆQDy

    A) TUB5ScQ&=\\ /35Z!!hE?ÆQDy
    B) TUB5ScQ&= / \35Z!!he?ÆQDy
    C) TUB5cQ &=\\ /35Z!!!hE?ÆQDy
    D) TUB5ScQ&=\\ /35Z!!he?ÆQDy

## FLEXIBILITY OF CLOSURE

FLEXIBILITY OF CLOSURE questions evaluate an aspiring officer's ability to recognize an object that is hidden within a pattern or series of larger objects. Accuracy is more important than speed for these questions. These questions tell the test takers exactly what they need to look for; the test takers must be able to take that information and find it within a larger pattern or series. In law enforcement, flexibility of closure is important because it allows officers to pinpoint a person or object within a larger scene. For instance, an officer may have to locate various escape routes within a larger scene or identify one person within a crowd.

**Examples**

```
I H N M N T I O P R D F Q S D R K N C Q S D J K O G Q J I L O P N M J
H F H Y T R E D C M J K L K U B H G Y F G T E D C F B M K I U W Q A S
X C G J Q J I L O P N M J H F H U J K H T R F D E D S Q Y T R E D C M J
K L K U N T I O P R D F Q S D R N J I Q N J U O L P R T O K E C F G H U
J K I L P Q T G J I K L N B F D K N C Q S D J K O G C B P L T G H U J K I
H N M N T I O P R D F Q S D R K N C Q S D J K O G C B D R N J I Q N J
U O L P R T O K E C F G H U J K I L P Q T G J I K L N B F D K N C Q S D
J K O G C B P L T G H U J K
```

14. How many *S*'s appear in the box above?
    A) 5
    B) 8
    C) 9
    D) 10

15. How many *J*'s appear in the box above?
    A) 10
    B) 12
    C) 20
    D) 22

# Answer Key

1. **B) Correct.** The line graph shows a gradual increase from 2014 to 2017, which is indicated by the upward slant of the line and the difference in data from 2014 and 2017. The number of murders in 2014, indicated by the first dot of the line graph from left to right, was roughly thirty. The number of murders in 2017 was closer to eighty. The movement from a lower number to a higher number shows an increase.

2. **C) Correct.** The murder rate plateaus, or flattens, from 2015 to 2016. This was likely the year that the program to fight against the murder rate was instituted. The increase in the rate from 2016 to 2017 logically indicates that that was likely the year the program was disbanded.

3. **A) Correct.** This choice follows the response orders recommended in the policy above: (1) "restore order by asserting control of the situation," (2) "identify and secure any weapons or objects that can be used as weapons," and (3a) "if medical assistance is needed, the law enforcement officer must call for an ambulance or arrange for the victim's transfer to a hospital." It also respects policy recommendation II.II: "If another department member is involved in the domestic incident, the responding member must request that a department member of higher rank be present."

4. **C) Correct.** According to policy II.I.3.a, "If the victim refuses treatment, the law enforcement officer must advise the victim of the importance of getting medical attention."

5. **D) Correct.** The "wheezing and bruising," especially when viewed through the perspective of the original call of a physical altercation, are documentable details that indicate a domestic violence case may have occurred. The boy's apology and claims about the video game might be untrue. The father holding the son's hand might be a sign of control, not comfort. The wheezing and bruising, however, are evidence of a possible injury.

6. **C) Correct.** The driver is specifically avoiding addressing the officer's question about his glove compartment. All the other answer choices simply address assumptions instead of details or facts. The facts state that the driver was fiddling around in his glove compartment, he is irritable and agitated, and he is ignoring questions. It is logical that he might be concealing something in the glove compartment. He may be impatient or dislike police officers, but that conclusion ignores the driver's failure to address the officer's questions about the glove compartment. Claiming the driver is intoxicated or hiding drugs is only an assumption because there is no evidence of alcohol or drugs; the officer does not smell alcohol or marijuana, nor does he observe drug paraphernalia.

7. **B) Correct.** There is no southbound, eastbound, or westbound road at this intersection. The only place to go is north toward Oak Boulevard. Since north

is the only logical first move by car, the cruiser has to then move east on Oak Boulevard, past City Hall, and south on Main Street, past the train station.

8. **C) Correct.** Pine Park is due east of Sycamore Apartments, according to the map. Thus, it is likely that the window was facing in that direction. If it were facing in any other direction, Pine Park would not be visible.

9. **C) Correct.** Causally and logically speaking, in reverse order, the bedroom door would have to be closed or locked (number 2) before it is kicked down (number 7), ruling out choice D. They would have to relocate upstairs first in order to even be in that space (number 1). There would have to be a reason to lock the door and run upstairs (number 6). The violent act would likely be rooted in anger (number 3). The anger would likely be rooted in an action/conflict/disagreement/statement (numbers 5 and 4). But the only logical causality of that conflict, at least in this case, is that there was an original claim (number 4) followed by a counterclaim (number 5).

10. **B) Correct.** There are two officers in the photo.

11. **C) Correct.** The officers are likely standing by the side of the road; a cruiser and motorcycle are pulled over, and they are standing by brush overlooking mountains.

12. **C) Correct.**

13. **C) Correct.**

14. **C) Correct.** The letter *S* appears nine times.

```
IHNMNTIOPRDFQSDRKNCQSDJKOGQJILOPNMJ
HFHYTREDCMJKLKUBHGYFGTEDCFBMKIUWQAS
XCGJQJILOPNMJHFHUJKHTRFDEDSQYTREDCMJ
KLKUNTIOPRDFQSDRNJIQNJUOLPRTOKECFGHU
JKILPQTGJIKLNBFDKNCQSDJKOGCBPLTGHUJKI
HNMNTIOPRDFQSDRKNCQSDJKOGCBDRNJIQNJ
UOLPRTOKECFGHUJKILPQTGJIKLNBFDKNCQSD
JKOGCBPLTGHUJK
```

15. **D) Correct.** The letter *J* appears twenty-two times.

```
IHNMNTIOPRDFQSDRKNCQSDJKOGQJILOPNMJ
HFHYTREDCMJKLKUBHGYFGTEDCFBMKIUWQAS
XCGJQJILOPNMJHFHUJKHTRFDEDSQYTREDCMJ
KLKUNTIOPRDFQSDRNJIQNJUOLPRTOKECFGHU
JKILPQTGJIKLNBFDKNCQSDJKOGCBPLTGHUJKI
HNMNTIOPRDFQSDRKNCQSDJKOGCBDRNJIQNJ
UOLPRTOKECFGHUJKILPQTGJIKLNBFDKNCQSD
JKOGCBPLTGHUJK
```

# PRACTICE TEST

## READING COMPREHENSION

On exams like the PELLETB, CJBAT, MCOLES, and more, reading comprehension tests measure a candidate's ability to read and understand various written materials. Read each paragraph or passage and choose the response that best answers the question. All questions are self-contained and use only information provided in the passage that precedes them.

(1) When people think critically, they examine, evaluate, and synthesize information they have gathered in order to arrive at a logical conclusion. Critical thinking can be accomplished at a simple or more probing level, depending on whether a cursory or more thoughtful conclusion is desired. At its most basic level, critical thinking is an activity necessary for people to function properly in society. Every day, without thought, most people engage in simple critical thinking exercises as they interact with one another. They observe, analyze, and assess clues and information around them in order to understand others' behavior and to make decisions about how to respond appropriately. When used purposefully, critical thinking can help one gain a much greater understanding of the gathered information. However, many people do not wish to move beyond this basic, instinctual level when deep critical thinking is not **imperative**. They do not wish to gain deeper understanding of a person or issue even though gaining such understanding may be as simple as asking, "Why?"

(2) Intensive critical thinking is employed most often in academic settings. Teachers challenge students to apply a higher order of thinking skills to avoid oversimplification, to be objective, and to always ask the next question such as "Why?" "What?" or "What if?" to make reasoned judgments. Critical thinking in academia generally requires a supposition, facts, and information, and the ability to infer a logical conclusion from one or more assertions. In academia, critical thinking can either be relegated to mere theoretical dialogue or be applied to an actual problem in order to generate improved conditions.

(3) Since the 1970s, critical thinking has also been used in police work. It is vital, purposeful, and systematic. Police must analyze crimes and criminal activity, establish facts, and determine what information remains unknown. Police investigators analyze patterns and evidence to determine how and why criminal activity was committed and who committed the crime. They ask the questions "What's missing?" "What are the benefits of the crime?" "Who benefited?" "Was the crime planned or opportunistic?" Each question probes deeper into the issue and helps investigators uncover clues to reconstruct other people's reasoning. Critical thinking in police work questions the known facts of a case in such a way that investigators are able to understand criminal actions, and those who commit them, more accurately. Such thinking can help investigators understand a perpetrator's state of mind, determine what the perpetrator was thinking, how

he or she was thinking, as well as establish the investigator's opinion of what, how, and why a particular event occurred.

(4) Recently, critical thinking has become even more vital to law enforcement because criminals continue to become more **savvy**. As technology has evolved, so has crime sophistication. Criminals have to work smarter to avoid being apprehended, thus detectives work smarter by studying, evaluating, and assessing evidence to successfully investigate and prosecute criminals.

1. The tone of the author can be best described as:
   (A) objective
   (B) argumentative
   (C) passionate
   (D) empathetic

2. As used in paragraph 1, what is the best synonym for *imperative*:
   (A) absolutely necessary
   (B) very important
   (C) of personal interest
   (D) avoidable

3. According to the passage, it can be inferred that the author believes which of the following:
   I. Critical thinking is used in many ways.
   II. Critical thinking is only important in academia.
   III. Critical thinking is vital in police work.
   (A) III only
   (B) II only
   (C) II and III only
   (D) I and III only

4. As used in paragraph 4, what is the best definition of *savvy*?
   (A) cool
   (B) shrewd
   (C) inexperienced
   (D) dangerous

5. Which of the following, if true, WEAKENS the main point of paragraph 3?
   (A) People do not use critical thinking in everyday life.
   (B) Law enforcement began using critical thinking methods in the 1990s.
   (C) Academics do not apply theory to real-life situations.
   (D) Critical thinking has reduced successful investigations and prosecutions of crimes.

6. What is the best title for this passage?
   (A) The Definition of Critical Thinking
   (B) Critical Thinking and Law Enforcement
   (C) The Many Applications of Critical Thinking
   (D) Critical Thinking: A Survey

7. According to the passage, what is the main reason for the application of critical thinking in police work?
   (A) to help investigators understand criminal activity and criminal perpetrators more accurately
   (B) to determine how criminal activity was committed and who committed the crime
   (C) because crime sophistication has evolved, and thus investigators must also evolve
   (D) all of the above

River City Police Department policy mandates that officers remain in good physical condition while employed with the department. Most officers would gladly comply, but commute times, long work hours, and mandatory overtime account for about fifteen hours of each officer's day. Officers recently asked River City about developing a wellness program for staff members, sworn staff in particular, including the ability to exercise in one of the many gyms located at various River City Police Department's satellite facilities. The resulting memo from the River City chief of police was disseminated to all staff.

Dear Staff,

It gives me great pleasure to work at an agency that is full of hardworking, motivated individuals, sworn and civilians alike, who seek new ways to continue improving themselves in both professional and personal life.

As you are aware, law enforcement is a physical job that requires the men and women who do the job to maintain a high level of physical fitness. I'm confident all of you would like to maintain that high level of physical fitness. I know this is difficult for many who have family obligations and long commutes from your respective homes in the outlying areas, and for those who work copious overtime shifts. These factors have undoubtedly created barriers for you to reach your personal goals and the required baseline goals of this department.

It was recently brought to my attention that a number of you requested permission to exercise at your duty station during your workday, on your meal break, in one of the various gyms we maintain on facility sites, in order to make exercising easier to fit into your daily routine. I understand your various dilemmas, but for reasons of liability, workers' compensation issues, as well as the logistical issues involved in managing meal breaks so an entire duty station is not working out at the same time, I must deny that request. I will, however, work with you in other ways to help you meet your fitness goals.

As of next week, the following policies will take effect under the River City Police Employee Wellness Pledge program:

- We will update our meal program for staff members assigned to duty stations where leaving base during shifts is disallowed. We will no longer provide hamburgers, soda, french fries, bacon, or chips. For those of you who work the night shift and eat breakfast, eggs and hash brown potatoes will still be available. If you would like to purchase a soda or snack during your twelve-hour shift, you may do so at the remaining vending machines on-site.
- You may not exercise at any gym during duty hours, even if you are on break. You are welcome to work out before or after your assigned shift at any of our gyms.
- We will begin a physical fitness club that will meet once a month at one of our facilities for organized workouts. This club is open to the first 30 people who sign up. I, as well as the **warriors** who already work out with me, would love for you to join us at our morning gym sessions.

Thank you for your diligence to do the job well and to make River City the best police department in the state. I look forward to helping you meet your fitness goals and to your feedback on this exciting new program.

Keep up the good work!

Sincerely,

– Chief Jeff Hyde

8. What is the main point of the chief's letter?
   (A) Physical fitness is important for police work.
   (B) The chief is willing to help officers and staff stay fit.
   (C) The chief does not want to be responsible for staff who exercise on duty.
   (D) It is primarily the responsibility of the employee to manage time for workouts.

9. What is the overall tone of the chief's letter?
   (A) cordial
   (B) angry
   (C) passionate
   (D) overbearing

10. What is the best meaning of the word *warriors* as used in the passage?
    (A) a person experienced in warfare
    (B) a person who shows great vigor
    (C) a person skilled in using weapons
    (D) a person with fitness experience

11. According to the chief, what is the main reason he denied the request to work out during work hours?
    (A) Staff should be working, not exercising.
    (B) Even though staff may be on break, River City is still liable for injuries.
    (C) It is difficult logistically to ensure not all staff are working out at the same time.
    (D) Both B and C are correct.

12. According to the passage, how many hours in a given day does the average River City officer have left to eat, sleep, run errands, and work out after he or she released from duty?
    (A) fifteen
    (B) seventeen
    (C) nine
    (D) eleven

These days, it is harder than ever for kids to simply "walk away" from a bully. Bullying among children and adolescents has evolved beyond taunting a smaller or less popular kid while he or she is at school, to cyberstalking children across city and state lines with the use of common electronic devices. Because of the increasing reach of bullies, among other things, suicides and violent confrontations among youth have risen over the years.

Because of the current scope of bullying, school administrators no longer rely solely on teachers to keep kids safe while at school. Rather, administrators build teams of collaborators that include health care workers, teachers, administration, security staff, and law enforcement personnel to ensure schools remain a safe place for kids to learn. School resource officers (SROs) receive training in issues that are unique to youth. Generally, SROs have an office on campus. They are stationed at the school and spend their time dealing with law enforcement issues. They also spend a great deal of time talking to kids about anything that interests them, such as school activities, sports, law enforcement, and life in general. Since SROs talk to kids at particular schools regularly, officers are in a unique position to identify emerging issues and prevent them before they develop into greater problems.

SROs play a large role in managing situations that involve bullying so that *all* involved students and families are heard and respected.

13. Which fact, if true, strengthens the author's main point?
    (A) More kids are bullied currently than in previous years.
    (B) The majority of bullying happens on school grounds.
    (C) Funding for school resource officers has been reduced.
    (D) Youth suicides are on the decline.

14. According to the passage, why are SROs important for managing bullying?
    (A) SROs arrest students who are too aggressive.
    (B) SROs get to know students and can prevent problems.
    (C) SROs provide defensive training for victims of bullies.
    (D) SROs help teachers learn to identify bullies.

15. According to the passage, why has bullying become so prevalent?
    (A) increased negative behavior
    (B) school resource officers on school grounds
    (C) technological advancement
    (D) boredom among children

With over twenty-two million staff members and students on college campuses across the nation, campus security has moved to the spotlight. Security staff have the opportunity to be proactive, educating the college community about campus life and being safe while in a home away from home.

Depending on the size and location of a given school, campus security staffing and scope might be either small-scale or **monolithically** entrenched in the campus community. Additionally, some campuses employ full-time police agencies, while others employ independent contractors or private security companies. However, because the nature and scope of each campus security department varies so widely, the level of communication with other security and law enforcement departments also varies, causing misunderstandings and errors in interdepartmental communication. Now is a crucial time, given the tragic events on school and college campuses and the sheer number of people continually on campuses, to begin creating universal standards so that all students and staff members have the same level of protection regardless of the school where they choose to study or work.

16. Which of the following, if true, most WEAKENS the argument that the variation in size and scope of campus security departments is the cause of communication problems?
    (A) Smaller operations have more money to spend on communications than large ones.
    (B) Interoperability between campuses is based on size and scope.
    (C) Each operation, regardless of size and scope, uses its own dedicated communication system.
    (D) Full-time police agencies have more capabilities than independent contractors.

17. Based on the tone of the passage, it can be inferred that the author believes which statement about campus security?
    (A) Campus security operations are varied to the point of dysfunction.
    (B) Size and scope do not necessarily matter if the operation functions properly.
    (C) Large campus security operations are safer than small ones.
    (D) Small campus security operations have better communications capabilities.

18. As used in the passage, what is the best definition of the word *monolithically*?
    (A) stonelike
    (B) impenetrable
    (C) massive
    (D) minuscule

19. According to the passage, what types of agencies are employed as campus security?
    (A) security companies
    (B) law enforcement
    (C) contractors
    (D) all of the above

20. According to the passage, what is an important problem that needs to be addressed?
    (A) communication among agencies
    (B) size of security agencies
    (C) education of the campus community
    (D) universal standards of protection

(1) Since the police usually do not have the opportunity to watch a crime as it happens, they must rely on evidence, statements from witnesses and involved parties, and deduction skills to draw conclusions about what actually occurred. Although reliance on information from others is essential, the information officers receive is often inaccurate either because the individual was mistaken in his or her perception, was biased, or was purposefully deceptive. Police must skillfully sift through all the information they receive and decide which is accurate and which is not. The officer's decision is generally based on his or

her assessment of the information's source and whether it is credible or reliable. There are three main reasons information is unreliable.

(2) The most frequent type of unreliable information is mistaken perception. Mistaken perception happens when otherwise honest and reliable people give information they believe to be true but is not. Mistaken perception can happen for a number of reasons. For example, during a stressful situation the brain releases adrenaline into the body, causing physiological changes. During periods of extreme stress, blood rushes away from nonessential organs and systems toward the heart. As this happens, people often experience various sensory disturbances, like time anomalies. Often witnesses and involved parties will report that a greater or lesser amount of time passed than actually did. A time **anomaly** affects an individual's sense of time, which appears to be moving at lightning speed or in slow motion. Sight and sound may also be affected. Witnesses and involved parties experiencing auditory occlusion often describe a temporary loss or lessening of hearing; sounds are muted or unheard. People also experience the feeling of tunnel vision, wherein peripheral vision is diminished and they can only see what is directly in front of them. People who undergo these physiological changes, even when mild, may have a distorted perception of the incident even though they are telling the truth based on their recollection. Police officers must pay attention to behavior cues that signal an individual may have altered perception due to physiological disturbances.

(3) Another issue with involved party reliability is individual bias. While some people have biases they are aware of, sometimes people have biases they are unaware of for a number of reasons. The bias may stem from accepting another source of information as true without question. In other words, the individual was uncritical of the information received and then passed along to police. People also may have a bias due to a vested interest in a particular view or outcome, and their perception is altered by that interest. Police officers must be diligent in identifying any possible biases during the interview process when establishing witness accuracy and reliability.

(4) Lastly, there are times when people are simply dishonest. The reason for their dishonesty may have nothing to do with the situation at hand. The motivation for the dishonesty may or may not be relevant to the incident, but it is crucial when determining the reliability of the statement itself. If a person is willing to be dishonest to the police, for whatever reason, his or her credibility must also be called into question. Police officers must pay attention to accounts of an incident by witnesses and involved parties for inconsistencies and **blatant** misinformation.

(5) There are many reasons why accounts of an incident by witnesses and involved parties might be unreliable. It is the officer's duty to use critical thinking, deduction, and logical reasoning to determine what is or is not reliable and why. Police officers have a variety of tools at their disposal in order to determine the accuracy of witness or involved party statements. Corroboration, witness expertise, police officer observations, evidence located at the scene, and the like, can help an officer analyze the information to determine the probable reliability of a statement.

**21.** The passage implies which of the following?

(A) Because witnesses are often unreliable, officers must be diligent in their investigation.

(B) Witnesses are never reliable; officers must use other evidence to prove crimes.

(C) The most frequent type of unreliable information is individual bias.

(D) Only some witnesses should be trusted, but it is impossible to tell who is reliable.

**22.** According to the passage, which of the following is true?

(A) People only lie for reasons related to the situation.

(B) Some people are unaware of bias they hold.

(C) During high-stress situations, blood rushes away from the heart.

(D) Witnesses' perception of time is generally quite accurate.

**23.** According to this article, what is the main reason for problems with witness reliability?

(A) dishonesty
(B) mistaken perception
(C) bias
(D) all of the above

**24.** What is the main point of this article?

(A) Witnesses are dishonest.
(B) Witnesses can be unreliable.
(C) Stress can alter witnesses' perception.
(D) Biased witnesses are unreliable.

**25.** According to the passage, what is auditory occlusion?

(A) total loss of hearing
(B) tunnel vision
(C) a temporary loss or lessening of hearing
(D) a sensory disturbance

**26.** What is the best synonym for the word *anomaly* as it is used in paragraph 2 of the passage?

(A) commonality
(B) ambivalence
(C) abnormality
(D) uncertainty

**27.** What word below is the best meaning of the word *blatant* as it is used in paragraph 4 of the passage?

(A) obvious
(B) flagrant
(C) subtle
(D) implied

---

(1) Think cattle rustling is a thing of the past? Think again. As of March 2014, cattle rustling in the western United States is still "a thing." Ranchers and law enforcement are **diligently** working together to protect herds and keep them safe from a brand-new threat—meth addicts. People addicted to methamphetamine have turned in their climbing boots and copper wire–grabbing gloves to steal cows in order to finance their drug habits. Where's the *Outlaw Josey Wales* when you need him?

(2) Levity aside, neither of the aforementioned issues is a laughing matter. Methamphetamine addiction is very serious, dangerous, and expensive to maintain. Issues surrounding the crime of cow theft is equally serious, dangerous, and expensive. Cows are valuable and can be sold at auction for around $1,000 a head. A local news station obtained video depicting thieves as they stole an entire pen of cows by coaxing them into the back of a big rig in the middle of the night. Another rancher had 100 cows stolen. At $1,000 a head, that's big money—and big jail time. Currently, cattle rustling carries penalties of up to ten years in prison. The problem for ranchers, while fortuitous for the thieves, is that it's fairly easy to avoid detection while selling stolen livestock at auction. Why? The cows often are not branded.

(3) Why not simply brand the cows? Well, that depends on the rancher. Some ranchers seek support and endorsements from the Certified Humane Project (CHP), and organizations like it, for meat products. CHP grades livestock on a step level from 1 to 5, with 1 being the lowest and 5 being the highest. The higher the meat's rating, the more natural, healthy, and flavorful it is, allowing the farmer to command a premium price. As farmers desire to return to natural and humane ways of farming and cattle raising, while also increasing their earnings potential, fewer farmers are branding their cattle. If farmers treat their animals humanely and get their animals' habitat closer to what normally occurs in nature, the meat will have a higher rating when it finally makes it to the grocery stores.

(4) One thing CHP has noted is that branding animals is not humane. As such, ranchers have a decision to make—protect the herd with brands or resist branding to achieve higher CHP step ratings. Either choice will likely cost them big bucks.

**28.** What is the main point of this passage?
- **(A)** Cows are expensive.
- **(B)** Cattle rustling is still a big problem for ranchers.
- **(C)** Ranchers should brand their cows.
- **(D)** Meat certifications are big money.

**29.** In paragraph 2, a rancher is said to have had 100 cows stolen. According to the article, what is the total monetary loss of the cows before processing?
- **(A)** $1,000,000
- **(B)** $10,000
- **(C)** $100,000
- **(D)** $1,000

**30.** According to the passage, what is a service that Certified Humane Project (CHP) provides?
- **(A)** third-party evaluation of farms and animal habitat
- **(B)** rate livestock and resultant meat products
- **(C)** create benchmarks for organic humane food sources
- **(D)** all of the above

**31.** The passage implies which is true about branding?
- **(A)** Branding does not affect the animals.
- **(B)** Branding is not a major issue for ranchers.
- **(C)** Ranchers make more money if they don't brand.
- **(D)** Most ranchers brand their cattle.

**32.** The passage mentions each of the following except _____.
- **(A)** Josey Wales, the outlaw
- **(B)** cattle rustling as "big money" for meth addicts
- **(C)** copper as a source for addicts to fund their habits
- **(D)** services for addicts to overcome addiction

**33.** Which of the words below most closely matches the meaning of the word *diligently* as used in the first paragraph?
- **(A)** neglectful
- **(B)** persistently
- **(C)** unconcerned
- **(D)** carefully

**34.** Which of the following is a central dilemma for ranchers?
- **(A)** It's easy to sell stolen cattle undetected because they are not branded, but branding the animals reduces their value.
- **(B)** Ranchers often know the addicts who steal their cattle because they are community and family members, making it difficult to prosecute them.
- **(C)** Branding cattle increases the value of the meat on the market, but it hurts the cows and is not humane.
- **(D)** The Certified Humane Project has been advocating to reduce meat consumption, making it difficult to sell beef.

---

(1) After a person convicted of a crime has served a sentence in a jail or prison, he or she is released back into the community. Prisoner release is a source of relief or frustration depending on individual perceptions, experience, and expectations. Some people believe a person who has committed a crime is lost and can never be **redeemed**. Others believe there are justifiable reasons why any given crime was committed, and thus very few people should go to jail or prison for extended times. Regardless of one's position, when a person has served a sentence, that individual will be released and will return to the community. Moreover, regardless of the opinions of others, the released person often has to deal with fear, confusion, and apprehension.

(2) So there are many questions that arise. Is it the responsibility of the community to support people who have violated the public trust as they re-enter society? And if so, how do communities support people newly released from jail so they do not become a statistic of recidivism? The answer to these questions forms the basis of re-entry programs throughout the nation.

(3) Generally speaking, most re-entry programs are composed of various community members and stakeholders. Collaboration between probation, parole, law enforcement, medical and mental health care workers, employment services, housing advocates, clergy, and a host of other services including substance abuse and domestic violence counseling are essential for making the transition smooth and successful. Collaborative partners ensure that resources are set up, or in motion, by the time of release so that participants do not find themselves homeless or re-entering a detrimental living situation immediately upon leaving prison.

(4) Re-entry programs have shown success in many communities. However, the perceived level of success may be well above or well below expectations, depending on individual **disposition**, the attitude of the participant, and the community in which they now live.

35. Based on the tone of this passage, which is it meant to do?
    (A) persuade
    (B) share information
    (C) admonish
    (D) stimulate thought

36. What is an appropriate title for this passage?
    (A) Community Frustrated Over Prisoner Release
    (B) Prisoner Re-entry Programs: What Happens Next
    (C) How to Decrease Recidivism Rates
    (D) Prisoner Re-entry

37. Based on the passage, it can be inferred that the author believes which of the following?
    (A) Criminals should never be let out of prison.
    (B) Many crimes are justified, and fewer people should receive long prison terms.
    (C) Community involvement is important for re-entry programs to work well.
    (D) Re-entry programs work.

38. As used in the last sentence, what is the best definition of the word *disposition*?
    (A) bad attitude
    (B) frustrations
    (C) positivity
    (D) natural inclination

39. What is the purpose of the second paragraph?
    (A) to illustrate the depth of the issue
    (B) to offer a supporting example
    (C) to avoid taking a position
    (D) to provide more details about the main idea

40. Which is the best synonym for the word *redeemed* as used in paragraph 1?
    (A) exchanged
    (B) converted
    (C) reformed
    (D) reclaimed

# WRITING

Police writing tests sometimes directly test your knowledge of grammar, sentence structure, and punctuation by asking you to identify errors or fill in the blank. Other tests will ask you to choose the more clearly written of two sentences. Most tests ask about spelling, and many test on vocabulary. This section provides a variety of questions to test your knowledge of good writing in Standard Written English.

## Grammar, Usage, and Structure

1. Choose the word or phrase that correctly completes the sentence.

   Because of its distance from the sun, the planet Neptune _____ that last the equivalent of forty-one Earth years.

   (A) have seasons
   (B) has seasons
   (C) have season
   (D) has season

2. Which of the following sentences does NOT contain an error?

   (A) The Iris and B. Gerald Cantor Roof Garden, atop the Metropolitan Museum of Art in New York City, offer a remarkable view.
   (B) The Mammoth-Flint Ridge Cave System, located in central Kentucky inside Mammoth Cave National Park, are the largest cave system in the world.
   (C) Andy Warhol's paintings, in addition to being the subject of the largest single-artist museum in the United States, are in great demand.
   (D) The field of child development are concerned with the emotional, psychological, and biological developments of infants and children.

3. Which of the following punctuation marks is used incorrectly?

   Ms. McIlvaine told her students that, although the Nile River, passes through eleven countries, it is the main water source of only two of them—Egypt and Sudan.

   (A) the comma after *that*
   (B) the comma after *River*
   (C) the comma after *countries*
   (D) the dash after *them*

4. Which of the following phrases contains an error in capitalization?

   The *Chicago Tribune* is famous for many reasons: in 1948, the paper published an erroneous headline about the winner of the Presidential election, and in 1974, it called for President Nixon's resignation.

   (A) *Chicago Tribune*
   (B) the paper
   (C) about the winner
   (D) Presidential election

5. Which of the following punctuation marks is used incorrectly?

   Our professor says that, though the term *nomad* is often associated with early populations, nomadic cultures exist today, especially in the mountain's of Europe and Asia.

   (A) the comma after *that*
   (B) the comma after *populations*
   (C) the comma after *today*
   (D) the apostrophe in *mountain's*

6. Choose the word or phrase that correctly completes the sentence.

   Engineers _____ seat belts to stop the inertia of traveling bodies by applying an opposing force on the driver and passengers during a collision.

   (A) designing
   (B) design
   (C) was designing
   (D) will have designed

7. Choose the word or phrase that most correctly completes the sentence.

   The employer decided that he could not, due to the high cost of health care, afford to offer _____ benefits to his employees.

   (A) for other
   (B) some other
   (C) no other
   (D) any other

8. Which of the following sentences does NOT have an error?

   (A) In addition to the disastrous effects an active volcano can have on it's immediate surroundings, an eruption can also pose a threat to passing aircraft.
   (B) In addition to the disastrous effects an active volcano can have on it's immediate surroundings: an eruption can also pose a threat to passing aircraft.
   (C) In addition to the disastrous effects an active volcano can have on its immediate surroundings: an eruption can also pose a threat to passing aircraft!
   (D) In addition to the disastrous effects an active volcano can have on its immediate surroundings, an eruption can also pose a threat to passing aircraft.

9. Choose the word or phrase that correctly completes the sentence.

   Though organized firefighting groups existed as early as Ancient Egypt, the first fully state-run brigade was created by Emperor Augustus of Rome _____ as the nation's official police force.

   (A) which also functioned
   (B) and also functioned
   (C) for also functioning
   (D) that also functioned

10. Which of the following punctuation marks is used incorrectly?

    In many European countries such as, France, Spain, and Italy, hot chocolate is made with real melted chocolate; this creates a beverage that is thick and rich.

    (A) the comma after *as*
    (B) the comma after *France*
    (C) the comma after *Italy*
    (D) the semicolon after *chocolate*

11. Choose the word or phrase that correctly completes the sentence.

    Though Puerto Rico is known for _____ beaches, its landscape also includes mountains, which are home to many of the island's rural villages.

    (A) its
    (B) it's
    (C) their
    (D) there

12. Which of the following sentences has an error?

    (A) Animals use estivation to avoid harsh conditions and to help it survive winter.
    (B) Some species of fish use luminescent lures to trick other fish into moving closer to them.
    (C) In a parasitic relationship, one species is negatively affected while the other species acquires what it needs to survive.
    (D) Tropical rainforests are made up of many layers, each of which has its own distinct species.

13. Which sentence does NOT contain an error?

    (A) The grandchildren and their cousins enjoyed their day at the beach.
    (B) Most of the grass has lost their deep color.
    (C) The jury was cheering as their commitment comes to a close.
    (D) Every boy and girl must learns to behave themselves in school.

14. Which of the following punctuation marks is used incorrectly?

    My dad told us something interesting: on Parents' Day, a public holiday in the Democratic Republic of Congo, families celebrate parents' both living and deceased.

    **(A)** the colon following *interesting*

    **(B)** the apostrophe in *Parents' Day*

    **(C)** the comma following *Day*

    **(D)** the apostrophe in *parents'*

15. Choose the word or phrase that correctly completes the sentence.

    In the fight against obesity, countries around the world _____ imposing taxes on sodas and other sugary drinks in hopes of curbing unhealthy habits.

    **(A)** is

    **(B)** did

    **(C)** are

    **(D)** were

16. Which of the following phrases follows the rules of capitalization?

    **(A)** President Carter and his advisers

    **(B)** Robert Jones, the senior Senator from California

    **(C)** my Aunt and Uncle who live out west

    **(D)** the party on New Year's eve

17. Choose the word or phrase that correctly completes the sentence.

    The storm chasers, who emphasized the importance of caution in _____ work, decided not to go out when the rain made visibility too low.

    **(A)** his

    **(B)** their

    **(C)** its

    **(D)** his or her

18. Which sentence does NOT contain an error?

    **(A)** My sister and my best friend lives in Chicago.

    **(B)** My parents or my brother is going to pick me up from the airport.

    **(C)** Neither of the students refuse to take the exam.

    **(D)** The team were playing a great game until the rain started.

19. Choose the word that correctly completes the sentence.

    The assassination of President John F. Kennedy _____ to haunt and fascinate Americans, with new movies, books, and television series still being released every year.

    **(A)** continue

    **(B)** continuing

    **(C)** continued

    **(D)** continues

20. Choose the word that correctly completes the sentence.

    The research organization includes members _____ fields of study span many disciplines, such as math, sciences, arts, humanities, public affairs, and business.

    **(A)** whose

    **(B)** who's

    **(C)** those

    **(D)** their

## Clarity

In the following sentence pairs, identify the sentence that is most clearly written.

1. (A) Julie was happy to get back to her life after the trial she felt she received justice.
   (B) Julie was happy to get back to her life after the trial. She felt she received justice.

2. (A) Marge told Ruth that Marge's supervisor wanted to speak with Ruth.
   (B) Marge told Ruth that her supervisor wanted to speak with her.

3. (A) Kelly did not see the cyclist riding in her blind spot, and she hit him with her car as she made the right turn.
   (B) Kelly did not see the cyclist riding in her blind spot, and she hit him with her car. As she made the right turn.

4. (A) Officers who train rarely are caught off guard.
   (B) Officers who train are rarely caught off guard.

5. (A) The defendant was angry at the sentence he received. He antagonized the judge out of frustration.
   (B) The defendant was angry at the sentence he received he antagonized the judge out of frustration.

6. (A) Police officers who keep up to date with changing laws, policies, and community priorities tend to be more successful than those who do not, unless they are assigned to special covert details that have little contact with ordinary citizens.
   (B) Police officers who keep up to date with changing laws, policies, and community priorities tend to be more successful. Than those who do not unless they are assigned to special covert details that have little contact with ordinary citizens.

7. (A) Jake and Ronald were playing cards when Ronald shot Jake. In the leg.
   (B) Jake and Ronald were playing cards when Ronald shot Jake in the leg.

8. (A) Community leaders and law enforcement officers often work together toward common goals. Proactive problem solving and preventing social discord are two such goals.
   (B) Community leaders and law enforcement officers often work together toward common goals proactive problem solving and preventing social discord are two such goals.

9. (A) Detective Sherman almost got convictions for every felony arrest he ever made.
   (B) Detective Sherman got convictions for almost every arrest he ever made.

10. (A) Family law courtrooms are among the most dangerous because emotions run high when dealing with family issues.
    (B) Family law courtrooms are among the most dangerous because emotions run high. When dealing with family issues.

11. (A) Kyle wanted to sing, dance, and act; it is what made him happy.
    (B) Kyle wanted to sing, dance, and act; participating in the arts is what made him happy.

12. (A) Peaceful protests are part of the fabric of America. Protests are only illegal when they become unlawful assemblies or riots.
    (B) Peaceful protests are part of the fabric of America protests are only illegal when they become unlawful assemblies or riots.

13. (A) While happily at work downtown, Marta's house was burglarized.
    (B) While Marta was happily at work downtown, her house was burglarized.

14. (A) Officers collected fingerprints on print cards.
    (B) Fingerprints were collected by officers on print cards.

15. (A) Fran was very afraid, but she kept her fear hidden.
    (B) Fran was very afraid, but she kept it hidden.

16. (A) The bus driver lost control of the bus while turning a corner. Too fast.
    (B) The bus driver lost control of the bus while turning a corner too fast.

17. (A) Steven saw his stolen car on the way to work.
    (B) On the way to work, Steven saw his stolen car.

18. (A) Jared drank several alcoholic beverages at the party. He crashed into a parked car on the way home and was arrested for DUI.
    B) Jared drank several alcoholic beverages at the party he crashed into a parked car on the way home and was arrested for DUI.

19. (A) Officer Daryn said he did not like to drive in pursuits because the fast speeds make you sick.
    B) Officer Daryn said he did not like to drive in pursuits because the fast speeds make him sick.

20. (A) Generally, most people remain unaware of the judicial system's process. Unless they become a party to an action.
    B) Generally, most people remain unaware of the judicial system's process unless they become a party to an action.

21. (A) As the defendant was remanded into custody, the judge lectured him.
    (B) The judge lectured the defendant as he was remanded into custody.

22. (A) Court clerks are essential members of the court staff they maintain all the court documents and record each word spoken in court while "on the record."
    (B) Court clerks are essential members of the court staff. They maintain all the court documents and record each word spoken in court while "on the record."

23. (A) Jack called the Sheriff's Office, but they did not return his call.
    (B) Jack called the Sheriff's Office, but the answering service did not return his call.

24. (A) Greg's neighbor has a dog. That barks all hours of the day and night.
    B) Greg's neighbor has a dog that barks all hours of the day and night.

25. (A) Officer Martinez reported the stolen car.
    (B) The car was reported stolen by Officer Martinez.

26. (A) Community policing is not a new concept it has, however, recently received a face-lift.
    (B) Community policing is not a new concept. It has, however, recently received a face-lift.

27. (A) Eagerly awaiting time off, Ebony's vacation was just about to start.
    (B) Eagerly awaiting time off, Ebony was just about to start her vacation.

28. (A) Stoplights are often timed for safety when drivers "jump" the green, they are cheating the system, and the results could be deadly.
    (B) Stoplights are often timed for safety. When drivers "jump" the green, they are cheating the system, and the results could be deadly.

29. (A) Inmates received lunches in bags from deputies.
    (B) Inmates received lunches from deputies in bags.

30. A) Every time Alonzo turned on the TV, they said another city was experiencing unrest.
    B) Every time Alonzo turned on the TV, the news reported another city was experiencing unrest.

**Vocabulary**

SYNONYMS

Choose a word from the answer choices that is CLOSEST in meaning to the underlined word.

1. Omari felt APATHETIC in his employment, so he decided to quit his job and go to law school.
   - (A) motivated
   - (B) dissatisfied
   - (C) indifferent
   - (D) unsure

2. After years of observing people in the worst situations of their lives, Austin's behavior became CALLOUS.
   - (A) mean
   - (B) insensitive
   - (C) annoyed
   - (D) empathetic

3. Cheryl was nervous, but she did not want to HINDER her daughter's dream of becoming a police officer.
   - (A) encourage
   - (B) expedite
   - (C) crush
   - (D) impede

4. Larry thought his neighbor, John, was PILFERING Larry's morning newspaper, so he reported him to the constable.
   - (A) stealing
   - (B) borrowing
   - (C) moving
   - (D) returning

5. Blanca had an INCONSPICUOUS scar on her arm from a car accident several years earlier.
   - (A) large
   - (B) prominent
   - (C) unnoticeable
   - (D) small

6. Hank was drunk and BELLIGERENT because his wife left him.
   - (A) hostile
   - (B) sad
   - (C) angry
   - (D) loud

7. Clyde was LUCID when he told the paramedics who shot him.
   - (A) confused
   - (B) rational
   - (C) emotional
   - (D) incomprehensible

8. Julian became FRANTIC when he realized his child was missing.
   - (A) frenzied
   - (B) calm
   - (C) frustrated
   - (D) upset

9. Henry only EXACERBATED the problem when he poured water on a grease fire.
   - (A) hurt
   - (B) reduced
   - (C) aggravated
   - (D) excited

10. Deputy Hanes writes reports that tend to be VERBOSE.
    - (A) concise
    - (B) clear
    - (C) confusing
    - (D) wordy

11. One purpose of community policing is to FOSTER relationships between the police and the communities they serve.
    - (A) alleviate
    - (B) create
    - (C) discourage
    - (D) promote

PRACTICE TEST 77

**12.** It is impossible to QUANTIFY the damage resulting from the fire.
  (A) measure
  (B) understand
  (C) extend
  (D) improve

**13.** The jury came to a DUBIOUS conclusion based on the evidence.
  (A) dishonest
  (B) questionable
  (C) obvious
  (D) definite

**14.** Officers FURTIVELY infiltrated the gang in order to gather intelligence.
  (A) stealthily
  (B) fraudulently
  (C) brazenly
  (D) openly

**15.** Deputy Wilson worked very hard to HONE her skills as an officer.
  (A) build
  (B) sharpen
  (C) steady
  (D) improve

### ANTONYMS

Choose a word from the answer choices that is most OPPOSITE the underlined word.

**1.** After working several twelve-hour shifts in a row, Deputy Nguyen developed a PERSISTENT cough.
  (A) lasting
  (B) intermittent
  (C) unrelenting
  (D) harsh

**2.** Case law sometimes SUPERSEDES legislated law and statutes.
  (A) supports
  (B) overrides
  (C) submits
  (D) boosts

**3.** If used successfully, the "heat of passion" defense can MITIGATE murder to manslaughter.
  (A) lessen
  (B) bolster
  (C) extend
  (D) change

**4.** Judge Singleton ABDICATED her seat on the bench because she was seriously ill.
  (A) left
  (B) maintained
  (C) abandoned
  (D) relinquished

**5.** The jury was admonished and advised that they could not DEVIATE from the instructions.
  (A) diverge
  (B) depart
  (C) sway
  (D) remain

**6.** Toby made his way to the top with GUILE and swindled thousands of people out of millions of dollars.
  (A) duplicity
  (B) assistance
  (C) honesty
  (D) savvy

**7.** Each year, many laws and statutes are REPEALED.
  (A) revoked
  (B) arranged
  (C) added
  (D) understood

**8.** The suspect DISAVOWED any knowledge of the crime.
  (A) admitted
  (B) wondered
  (C) dismissed
  (D) refused

FILL IN THE BLANK

The following questions provide two word choices to complete the sentences below. Choose the word that makes the most sense based on the context of the sentence.

1. The tactical commander outlined the _____ of action for the SWAT team.
   (A) coarse
   (B) course

2. The nightly news reported that the police apprehended the _____ killer who had been tormenting River City residents.
   (A) cereal
   (B) serial

3. Increased penalties for criminal activity in River City did not appear to have an _____ on the occurrence of crime.
   (A) effect
   (B) affect

4. When Tom spoke at the town hall meeting, he intended his words to motivate people to fight for their rights, not to _____ a riot.
   (A) incite
   (B) insight

5. Mayor Brighton did not _____ whether Oscar's speech was protected by the First Amendment of the Constitution.
   (A) know
   (B) no

6. Jerry had not eaten in four days and had no money, so he decided to _____ some food to get by.
   (A) steel
   (B) steal

7. While on the job, it is our duty to uphold the _____ of good policing.
   (A) principles
   (B) principals

## Spelling

CHOOSE THE CORRECT SPELLING

Read the following sentences and choose the correct spelling of the missing word.

1. The jury foreman turned _____ the defendant when he read the verdict.
   (A) tward
   (B) toword
   (C) toward
   (D) tword

2. The District Attorney _____ dropped off the case files this morning.
   (A) leason
   (B) liason
   (C) laison
   (D) liaison

3. The legislature _____ the law when it was ruled unconstitutional.
   (A) resinded
   (B) recinded
   (C) rescinded
   (D) resended

4. Even the defendant was _____ when the jury returned a not guilty verdict.
   (A) surprised
   (B) suprised
   (C) supprised
   (D) surprized

PRACTICE TEST   79

5. Officer Jones had a _____ to speak loudly, which often upset people.
   - (A) tendancy
   - (B) tendency
   - (C) tendencie
   - (D) tendincy

6. Officer uses of force are _____ and appropriate actions when suspects fail to comply and can escalate police contacts in a manner that jeopardizes safety.
   - (A) necessary
   - (B) nesisarry
   - (C) necassery
   - (D) necissary

7. John Smith told the court he did not recognize the authority of the _____ and was filing a lawsuit against it to reclaim money owed him as a right of birth.
   - (A) goverment
   - (B) govermant
   - (C) govirnment
   - (D) government

8. The tension in the courtroom was _____ as the jury prepared to read the verdict.
   - (A) palpible
   - (B) palpable
   - (C) palpebal
   - (D) palpabal

9. The suspect was _____ for four hours before he confessed.
   - (A) interrogated
   - (B) interogated
   - (C) interragated
   - (D) interagated

10. Four _____ witnesses placed Harry at the scene of the crime.
    - (A) indapendant
    - (B) independent
    - (C) independant
    - (D) indapendent

11. The judge signed a _____ to compel the company to turn the phone records over to the police.
    - (A) supena
    - (B) suppena
    - (C) subpoena
    - (D) supeana

12. Judy was _____ of her son, who suddenly had a lot of money and rarely came home at night.
    - (A) suspisious
    - (B) suspisios
    - (C) suspiscious
    - (D) suspicious

13. At the scene of a car accident, Officer Garcia attempted to _____ the exchange of information between drivers because they were arguing with each other.
    - (A) fasilitate
    - (B) fascilitate
    - (C) facilitate
    - (D) facilatate

14. As a victim of a _____ crime, Luis devoted his time to changing legislation regarding victims' rights.
    - (A) heinous
    - (B) hanous
    - (C) haneous
    - (D) hienous

15. Gabriel was an _____ child who would not listen to his parents and continued to get into trouble.
    - (A) incorrigable
    - (B) inccorigable
    - (C) incorrigeable
    - (D) incorrigible

16. Stella survived her attack because she was _____.
    - (A) tenacious
    - (B) tinasious
    - (C) tenasious
    - (D) tanancious

80 Police Officer Exam Study Guide

**17.** Officer Sasser knew the importance of attention to detail and never performed her duties in a _____ manner.
   (A) perfunctary
   (B) perfunctory
   (C) perfunctiry
   (D) perfunctery

**18.** Sovereign citizens are people who belong to a _____ organization and refuse to recognize the authority of the United States.
   (A) seditious
   (B) seditiuos
   (C) saditious
   (D) siditious

**19.** The president of the neighborhood watch called the police and requested a house be placed under _____ because its occupants were suspected of drug dealing.
   (A) survailance
   (B) surveillance
   (C) survielance
   (D) servielance

**20.** Ed was arrested for _____ because he was drunk and sleeping on a park bench at two o'clock in the afternoon.
   (A) vagrency
   (B) vagrincie
   (C) vagrincy
   (D) vagrancy

### IDENTIFYING SPELLING ERRORS

Choose the misspelled word. Only one word is misspelled in each sentence.

**1.** Sasha filed a restraining order against her ex-boyfriend because he was harrassing her at work.
   (A) restraining
   (B) against
   (C) because
   (D) harrassing

**2.** Pursuant to federal and state laws, all jails and prisons make reasonable accommadations for inmates who have disabilities to ensure they have the same or comparable access as inmates who do not have disabilities.
   (A) Pursuant
   (B) federal
   (C) accommadations
   (D) comparable

**3.** Bystanders were noticably upset after witnessing such a horrific accident.
   (A) Bystanders
   (B) noticably
   (C) horrific
   (D) accident

**4.** Jason was arrested because he was in possesion of stolen property.
   (A) arrested
   (B) because
   (C) possesion
   (D) property

**5.** River City Police Department found itself under seige after an officer, who was chasing a dangerous criminal, crashed his patrol car into a storefront during business hours.
   (A) seige
   (B) dangerous
   (C) storefront
   (D) business

**6.** At his sentencing, Jim publically apologized for his role in the home invasion robbery.
   (A) sentencing
   (B) publically
   (C) apologized
   (D) invasion

7. People who are under the influence of certain drugs can become stronger, more unpredictable, and more agressive than an average person.
   - (A) influence
   - (B) stronger
   - (C) unpredictable
   - (D) agressive

8. Andrea worked long hours as a court reporter and often suffered headaches from extended exposure to flourescent lighting.
   - (A) suffered
   - (B) headaches
   - (C) exposure
   - (D) flourescent

9. The relationship of the prosecution and the defense is advirsareal by design.
   - (A) prosecution
   - (B) defense
   - (C) advirsareal
   - (D) design

10. The judge ruled the information was not germain to the case and was thus inadmissible.
    - (A) judge
    - (B) germain
    - (C) thus
    - (D) inadmissible

## Cloze

Some police tests, like the PELLETB, have a cloze portion. On the cloze, fill in each blank with the appropriate word. The words are indicated by blank spaces and dashes within the passage. Each dash represents a letter. The word must be correct, given the context of the passage, and it must have the same number of letters as dashes. All words that meet both criteria are considered correct. More than one word may be appropriate for a given space.

### Cloze One

More than twenty-five years ago, law enforcement first partnered with community leaders in an attempt to bridge the gap between the police and the communities they serve. Law enforcement had long since realized _ _ _ _ _ _ _ _ changes were making it more and _ _ _ _ difficult to do the job without _ _ _ _ _ _ _ _ support. Because police could not do _ _ _ job alone, and thus did the _ _ _ poorly in certain communities, community trust _ _ _ _ _ to falter. The creation of community _ _ _ _ _ _ _ _ programs was a way to rebuild _ _ _ community trust as well as to reinvigorate _ _ and allow police to do their _ _ _ better. Initial community policing programs were _ _ _ _ _ _ _ _ _ designed to help community members mobilize _ _ _ _ _ _ _ and resources to solve problems, voice _ _ _ _ _ concerns, contribute advice, and take action _ _ address concerns. But these initial programs tended to be paternalistic, and while some _ _ _ _ _ _ _ _ _ _ _ showed improvement, the improvement was slow. _ _ other communities, residents and leaders outright _ _ _ _ _ _ _ _ the efforts of the police to _ _ _ _ together.

Over the years, community policing _ _ _ _ _ _ _ _. This evolution reflected moving away from the paternalism of _ _ _ programs and toward more true collaboration. _ _ _ _ _ _ than simply "voicing opinions," which police _ _ _ _ took under advisement while determining an action _ _ _ _, community members became bona fide stakeholders _ _ _ _ equal control over community priorities and _ _ _ _ _ _ plans. Today, community policing exists as _ collaborative effort between police and these community _ _ _ _ _ _ _ _ _ _ _ _ such as schools, community-based organizations, local large and small _ _ _ _ _ _ _ _ _ _, local government, and residents, and is designed to _ _ _ _ _ _ _ _, prioritize, and solve community problems. Across the United States, the _ _ _ _ _ _ _ _ _ community policing philosophy promotes organizational strategies _ _ _ _ use this collaboration to problem-solve _ _ _ proactively address persistent or emerging public _ _ _ _ _ _ problems such as crime and social _ _ _ _ _ _ _. All current community programs must be _ _ _ _ _ on three essential components:

82  Police Officer Exam Study Guide

\_ \_ \_ \_ \_ \_ \_ \_ \_ \_ \_ \_ partnerships; organizational transformation to support these collaborative partnerships as well as to support \_ \_ \_ \_ \_ \_ \_-solving methods; and a proactive, systemic \_ \_ \_ \_ \_ \_ \_ \_ \_ \_ of identified issues. This examination should also explore effective response evaluation. As a \_ \_ \_ \_ \_ \_ \_, models of community policing exist in most police agencies across the nation and the communities they serve, crisis situations have decreased in many communities, and the police have a markedly improved relationship with the citizens they \_ \_ \_ \_ \_.

## Cloze Two

All law enforcement officers are sworn in to the office using a standard oath. Each new officer proudly swears that \_ \_ or she will never betray his \_ \_ her badge, integrity, character, or the \_ \_ \_ \_ \_ \_ trust, and to uphold all laws \_ \_ \_ the United States Constitution. Every officer \_ \_ \_ \_ \_ this oath seriously. Most officers will never \_ \_ \_ \_ \_ \_ the day that badge was handed \_ \_ them and they raised their right \_ \_ \_ \_.

The oath is not the only \_ \_ \_ \_ \_ \_ \_ \_ an officer makes every day he or she \_ \_ \_ \_ on the badge. At each agency there \_ \_ \_ daily reminders of core values, traditions, \_ \_ \_ \_ \_ \_ \_ \_ rules, the police officers' prayer, and \_ \_ on. The tenets of each are fairly the same and give an officer \_ sense of pride about the job. \_ \_ \_ \_ \_ \_ \_ \_ such promise is the police officer \_ \_ \_ \_ of ethics. The officer code of \_ \_ \_ \_ \_ \_ takes the promise a little further, \_ \_ \_ \_ from the law and toward a \_ \_ \_ \_ humanitarian purpose. In the code of \_ \_ \_ \_ \_ \_, an officer affirms that his or her "fundamental duty" \_ \_ to serve humankind, to defend the \_ \_ \_ \_ and defenseless against oppression or intimidation, \_ \_ \_ the peaceful against violence and disorder.

It is this last sentence that \_ \_ most striking. In the midst of \_ \_ \_ \_ \_ \_ around the nation, many might assume \_ \_ \_ officers' role is to intimidate and \_ \_ \_ \_ \_ \_ \_ \_ rather than to prevent. Is \_ \_ possible then for chaos, violence, and \_ \_ \_ \_ \_ \_ \_ \_ to coexist with peacefulness in the \_ \_ \_ \_ space, such that any attempt to address violence will not necessarily and negatively \_ \_ \_ \_ \_ \_ the peaceful?

And, if so, how \_ \_ it possible for an officer to \_ \_ \_ \_ \_ \_ to the oath and the code? \_ \_ \_ \_ \_ \_ \_ \_, maybe there are two sides to \_ \_ \_ proverbial coin, and both sides of \_ \_ \_ truth are true, even if they may seem to conflict. Meanwhile, \_ \_ \_ can only hope for guidance. We hope also that as we attempt to navigate issues of violence, peace, civil disobedience, and \_ \_ \_ \_ \_ \_ disorder amid the anger, frustration, and mistrust for one another, officers will continue to remember the overwhelming pride and honor felt the day that badge was handed to them, they raised their \_ \_ \_ \_ \_ hand, and \_ \_ \_ \_ \_ always to do the right thing.

# MATHEMATICS

Police tests sometimes directly test your knowledge of mathematics. Most questions revolve around arithmetic (mathematical operations), working with percentages and decimals, ratios and proportions, estimation and rounding, units, and space (area and perimeter). This section provides a variety of questions to test your knowledge of mathematics

## Mathematical Operations

1. An elderly woman had her purse stolen. Inside the purse, she had 6 twenty-dollar bills, 3 ten-dollar bills, and 4 one-dollar bills. How much money did she have stolen altogether?
   - (A) $154
   - (B) $164
   - (C) $174
   - (D) $184

2. A case of ammunition contains 20 boxes of bullets. Each box contains 100 bullets. How many bullets are in each case?
   - (A) 200
   - (B) 1000
   - (C) 1500
   - (D) 2000

3. The traffic department wrote 240 speeding tickets last month. Eight officers make up the traffic department. Assuming each officer wrote the same number of tickets, how many tickets were written per officer?
   - (A) 20
   - (B) 25
   - (C) 30
   - (D) 35

4. When working on the weekends, new police officers receive a weekend bonus of $50 plus $22 per hour. If an officer worked 4 hours on the weekend, how much money would she earn?
   - (A) $122
   - (B) $138
   - (C) $140
   - (D) $146

5. At the end of each year a police officer receives an evaluation with a score from 1 to 100. For each demerit, 7 points are lost. Which statement below represents the effect of having 3 demerits toward your evaluation?
   - (A) $3 \times 7 = 21$
   - (B) $3 \times -7 = -21$
   - (C) $-3 \times -7 = -21$
   - (D) $-3 \times -7 = 21$

6. The temperature at the start of your shift is −15°F. The temperature is forecast to drop 8 more degrees. If this is true, what will be the low temperature for the day?
   - (A) −23°F
   - (B) −7°F
   - (C) −30°F
   - (D) −9°F

7. The fine for speeding is $235. The fine for running a stop sign is $178. How much more is the fine for speeding than the fine for running a stop sign.
   - (A) $51
   - (B) $53
   - (C) $57
   - (D) $62

## Fractions, Decimals, and Percentages

1. Twenty grams of drugs were collected at the crime scene. Seven grams of each drug can be placed in each container. How many containers will be filled?
   - (A) $2\frac{6}{7}$ containers
   - (B) $2\frac{3}{7}$ containers
   - (C) $3\frac{1}{7}$ containers
   - (D) $3\frac{6}{7}$ containers

2. Officer Larson's paycheck was $340. She pays 15 percent in federal taxes. How many dollars will she pay in federal taxes?
   - (A) $49
   - (B) $51
   - (C) $55
   - (D) $60

3. A flashlight weighs $2\frac{3}{4}$ pounds. A belt weighs $1\frac{7}{8}$ pounds. How much heavier is the flashlight than the belt?
   - (A) $\frac{3}{8}$ pounds
   - (B) $\frac{7}{8}$ pounds
   - (C) $1\frac{7}{8}$ pounds
   - (D) $\frac{5}{16}$ pounds

4. The cost of a speeding ticket is $230.50. The cost of a parking violation is $187.90. How much more is the cost of a speeding ticket?
   - (A) $40.60
   - (B) $40.80
   - (C) $42.40
   - (D) $42.60

5. Officer Smith measured the distance of the crime scene to be $2\frac{1}{2}$ miles wide. Three-fourths of that distance has already been examined. What is the remaining width to be examined?
   - (A) 1 mile
   - (B) $\frac{3}{8}$ mile
   - (C) $\frac{1}{2}$ mile
   - (D) $\frac{5}{8}$ mile

6. There are 150 lbs. of ammunition that must be divided into pouches that contain a third of a pound of ammunition. How many pouches can be made?
   - (A) 50
   - (B) 150
   - (C) 450
   - (D) 500

7. At the Brookside Diner, Officer Mendez ordered a sandwich for $4.50, a drink for $1.45, and a bowl of soup for $2.45. How much was the total?
   - (A) $8.40
   - (B) $8.55
   - (C) $8.70
   - (D) $8.80

## Ratios and Proportions

1. There are 70 police officers in the local precinct. Forty of the officers are men. What is the ratio of men to women?
   - (A) 4:3
   - (B) 3:4
   - (C) 3:7
   - (D) 7:4

2. There were 300 arrests made last month. Fifty of the arrests were for disorderly conduct. What is the ratio of arrests for disorderly conduct to arrests for other offenses?
   - (A) 1:5
   - (B) 3:25
   - (C) 5:17
   - (D) 2:125

3. At the academy, there are 50 cadets. Twenty of them have children. What is the ratio of cadets with children to cadets without children?

   (A) 3:5
   (B) 1:5
   (C) 2:3
   (D) 2:5

4. If Officer O'Malley can patrol 7 blocks in 30 minutes, how long would it take him to patrol 10 blocks at the same rate?

   (A) About 40 minutes
   (B) About 43 minutes
   (C) About 47 minutes
   (D) About 50 minutes

5. The ratio of men to women in the local station is 5:8. If there are 120 women, how many men would there be?

   (A) 72 men
   (B) 74 men
   (C) 75 men
   (D) 77 men

6. The cost to buy 7 gallons of gasoline is $17.50. What would be the cost to buy 12 gallons of gasoline?

   (A) $28
   (B) $28.45
   (C) $29.50
   (D) $30

## Estimation and Rounding

1. The cost of Alex's gun was $441.78, and the cost of his uniform was $178.12. What is the best estimation for the cost of the two items?

   (A) $590
   (B) $600
   (C) $620
   (D) $700

2. The cost of new brakes on a police car is $245.90. What is the best estimation of the cost of getting new brakes on 4 cars?

   (A) $1000
   (B) $1200
   (C) $800
   (D) $900

3. Sally paid $45.89 in federal taxes, $17.90 in state taxes, and $5.78 in local taxes. Estimate the total amount of taxes that she paid.

   (A) $70
   (B) $85
   (C) $90
   (D) $100

4. The cost of Officer Henderson's vest was $283.96, and the cost of her belt was $38.12. Estimate the total cost of the 2 items.

   (A) $290
   (B) $300
   (C) $310
   (D) $320

5. The total budget for the police station is $145,893.45 for this year. What is this value rounded to the nearest thousand?

   (A) $145 thousand
   (B) $146 thousand
   (C) $147 thousand
   (D) $1350 thousand

6. Office Hoppert's total salary for last year came to $61,370.54. What is this amount rounded to the nearest hundred?

   (A) $61,300
   (B) $61,400
   (C) $61,000
   (D) $62,000

## Units

1. Kendra runs 2 miles every day to prepare for the police physical fitness test. How many yards does she run?
   - (A) 3290 yds
   - (B) 3340 yds
   - (C) 3400 yds
   - (D) 3520 yds

2. The weight of the average police dog is 35 lbs. How many ounces is this?
   - (A) 490 oz
   - (B) 510 oz
   - (C) 560 oz
   - (D) 570 oz

3. The SWAT team's truck can transport up to 1.2 tons of equipment. How many pounds is this?
   - (A) 2200 lbs
   - (B) 2400 lbs
   - (C) 2600 lbs
   - (D) 2800 lbs

4. The annual Policeman's Charity 5K is going to be held this weekend. Five kilometers is how many meters?
   - (A) 50 m
   - (B) 500 m
   - (C) 5000 m
   - (D) 50,000 m

5. An inmate was sentenced to five and half years in prison. How many days is this? Assume that there are 30 days per month.
   - (A) 1800
   - (B) 1840
   - (C) 1880
   - (D) 1980

6. Officer Jenkins ran his 2-mile test in 17 minutes. What was his speed in miles per hour?
   - (A) about 7 miles per hour
   - (B) about 9 miles per hour
   - (C) about 11 miles per hour
   - (D) about 13 miles per hour

7. Detective Barnes discovered 1700 grams of cocaine at the crime scene. How many kilograms of cocaine is this?
   - (A) 1.7
   - (B) 17
   - (C) 170
   - (D) 170,000

## Perimeter and Area

1. In a rectangular-shaped crime scene, the width was 40 yards and the length was 70 yards. What is the area of the crime scene?
   - (A) 2400 sq yd
   - (B) 2700 sq yd
   - (C) 2800 sq yd
   - (D) 3800 sq yd

2. The logo for the police department contains a triangle with a height of 3 cm and a base of 5 cm. What is the area of the triangle?
   - (A) 6 cm$^2$
   - (B) 7.5 cm$^2$
   - (C) 10 cm$^2$
   - (D) 15 cm$^2$

3. The running track at the academy is circular. The diameter of the track is 170 yards. What is the distance around the track?

   (A) about 533.8 yards
   (B) about 633.8 yards
   (C) about 733.8 yards
   (D) about 833.8 yards

4. A square city block has an area of 40,000 square yards. What is length of one side of the block?

   (A) 200 yards
   (B) 400 yards
   (C) 1000 yards
   (D) 2000 yards

5. In the logo for the police department, there is a regular pentagon. Each side measures 5.1 cm. What is the perimeter of the pentagon?

   (A) 20.5 cm
   (B) 25 cm
   (C) 25.1 cm
   (D) 25.5 cm

6. The annual Police vs Fire Department football game is going to be played next week. The football field measures 100 yards by 30 yards. What is the perimeter of the football field?

   (A) 130 yards
   (B) 260 yards
   (C) 280 yards
   (D) 3000 yards

7. Chief Chen's office is in the shape of a rectangle with a width of 10 feet and a length of 12 feet. What is the area of his office?

   (A) 90 ft$^2$
   (B) 100 ft$^2$
   (C) 120 ft$^2$
   (D) 140 ft$^2$

# REASONING

Many police tests contain different types of reasoning questions. In this section, practice your reasoning, analytical, and visualization skills.

**Inductive Reasoning**

Read the graph below to answer the following five questions.

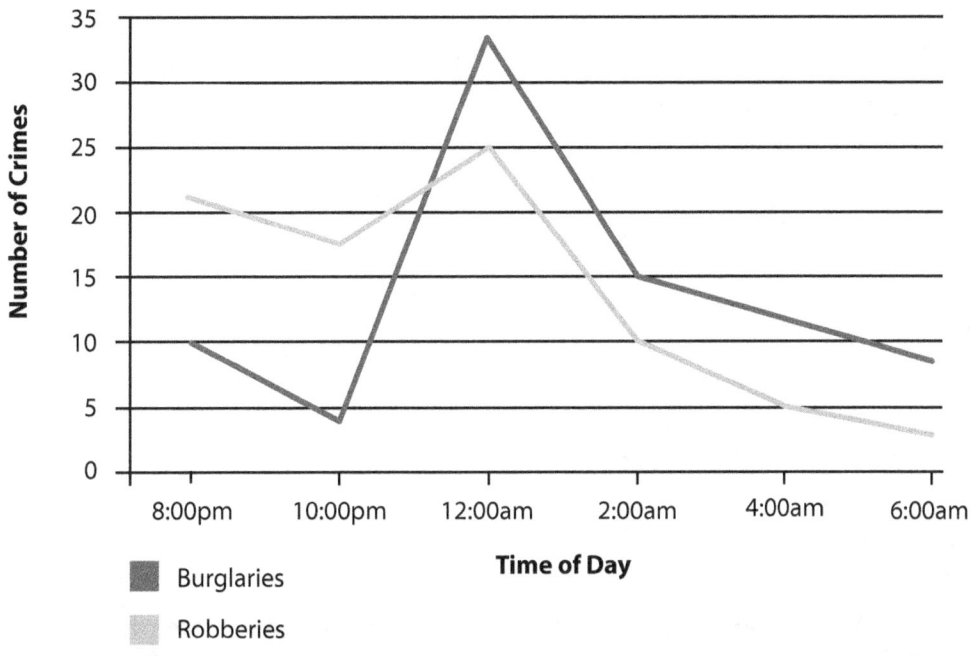

1. Some law enforcement officials blame an increase in all nightly crimes on the local bars closing at the same time. If this spike in crime is related to intoxicated patrons leaving the bars, what is the MOST LIKELY time that all the bars close?

    (A) 12:00 a.m.
    (B) 1:00 a.m.
    (C) 2:00 a.m.
    (D) 3:00 a.m.

2. Crime decreases at the sharpest rate during the night when the most police officers are on duty. In which time frame are most police officers MOST LIKELY patrolling?

    (A) between 8:00 p.m. and 10:00 p.m.
    (B) between 10:00 p.m. and 12:00 a.m.
    (C) between 12:00 a.m. and 2:00 a.m.
    (D) between 2:00 a.m. and 4:00 a.m.

3. Officer Wilkins can begin his shift anytime between 8:00 p.m. and 6:00 a.m. He wants to start at a time when robberies and burglaries are, on average, at their lowest. Which is the BEST time for the start of Officer Wilkins's shift?

    (A) 8:00 p.m.
    (B) 10:00 p.m.
    (C) 4:00 a.m.
    (D) 6:00 a.m.

4. A shift change occurs between 8:00 p.m. and 12:00 a.m., during which criminal activity temporarily decreases. Which of the following is MOST LIKELY the start time of this shift change?

    (A) 8:00 p.m.
    (B) 9:00 p.m.
    (C) 10:00 p.m.
    (D) 11:00 p.m.

PRACTICE TEST  89

5. Part-time officers have been hired to help out with the night shift. They can work any four-hour shift between 8:00 p.m. and 6:00 a.m. Which shift would encounter the FEWEST burglaries and robberies, on average?

   (A) 8:00 p.m. to 12:00 a.m.
   (B) 10:00 p.m. to 2:00 a.m.
   (C) 12:00 a.m. to 4:00 a.m.
   (D) 2:00 a.m. to 6:00 a.m.

The next five questions refer to the graph below.

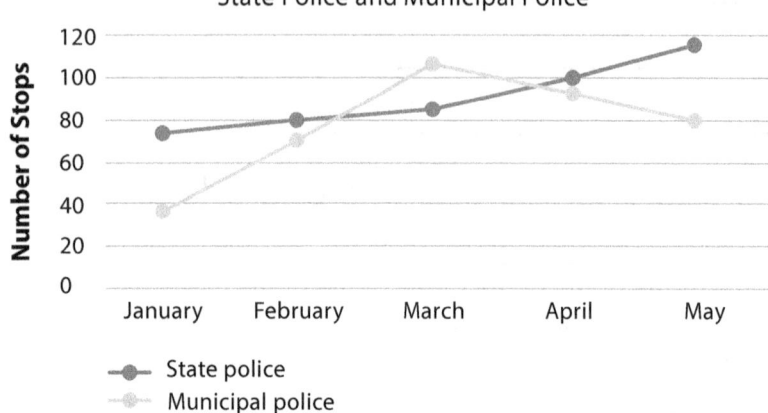

6. Sometime within the first five months of the year, Sergeant Michaels of the state police began an experimental initiative to maintain a quota of around eighty stops per month. What is the MOST LIKELY time frame for this quota?

   (A) January through March
   (B) February through April
   (C) March through April
   (D) February through May

7. Fearing the spring thaw might lead to an increase in speeding, the state police and municipal police began working together in Washington County to maintain a quota of around one hundred stops. In which month did this joint effort MOST LIKELY take place?

   (A) February
   (B) March
   (C) April
   (D) May

8. In an effort to "get on the same page" regarding the county's speeding issues, the state police and municipal police collaborated on plans to conduct speeding stops for two out of the first five months. Which two months show the greatest amount of collaboration between the state police and municipal police?

   (A) January and February
   (B) February and May
   (C) January and April
   (D) February and April

9. State patrol stops climbed to an all-time high during one of the first five months of the year because a fugitive was on the loose in Washington County. Which month MOST LIKELY represents this scenario?

   (A) February
   (B) March
   (C) April
   (D) May

10. An unexpected severe blizzard, which led to a state of emergency, was responsible for a five-month low for municipal stops. In which month did this blizzard MOST LIKELY occur?

    (A) January
    (B) February
    (C) March
    (D) April

Refer to the graph below to answer the following five questions.

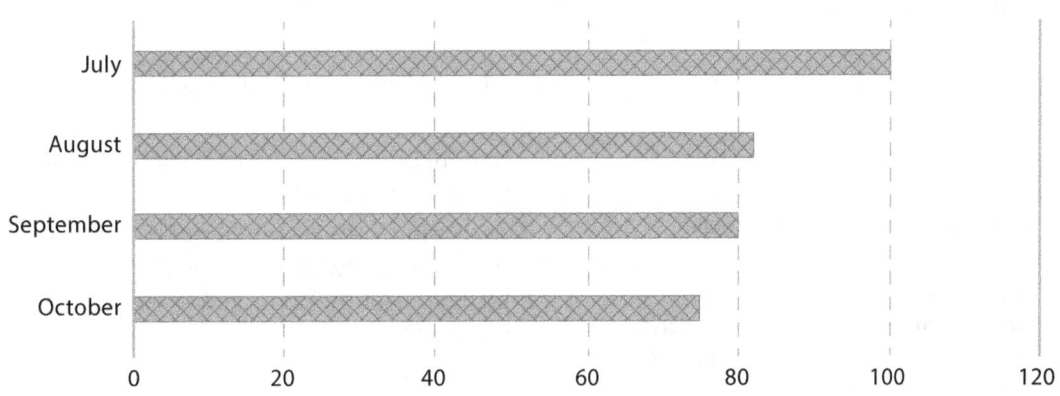

11. After noticing an all-time high of DUI incidents, state police began a new campaign to implement more DUI checkpoints, which led to a sharp decrease in DUIs. In which month did this initiative MOST LIKELY begin?

    (A) July
    (B) August
    (C) September
    (D) October

12. A sergeant in the state police force is gathering data for a news report about the results of the DUI checkpoint initiative. The sergeant wants to show the total decrease from the highest to lowest number of DUI cases as evidence of the initiative's effectiveness. What is the CLOSEST representation of the total decrease in incidents, according to the graph above?

    (A) an eighteen-incident decrease
    (B) a twenty-incident decrease
    (C) a twenty-four–incident decrease
    (D) a thirty-two–incident decrease

13. When were the most DUI incidents?

    (A) July
    (B) August
    (C) September
    (D) October

14. The state patrol set a goal to reduce DUI incidents below eighty. When did the state patrol MOST LIKELY focus on this goal?

    (A) July
    (B) August
    (C) September
    (D) October

15. A checkpoint off Interstate 94 was implemented for two out of the four months, leading to more consistent data on the number of DUIs. When was this checkpoint MOST LIKELY implemented?

    (A) July and August
    (B) July and September
    (C) August and September
    (D) September and October

PRACTICE TEST   91

## Deductive Reasoning

Questions 1 – 3 refer to the following passage.

Section 10. Whenever a police officer is ordered to appear before a board of captains as directed by the chief in accordance to State Code, the following procedures shall apply:

1. The hearing shall be conducted at a reasonable hour, and the office shall receive proper notice to appear.
2. The hearing shall take place either in the chief's conference room or an equivalent setting as designated by the board of captains.
3. Prior to such hearing, the officer shall be provided a Statement of Rights.
4. Hearing sessions shall be for reasonable periods of time and shall allow for personal necessities and rest periods as are reasonably necessary.
5. The board of captains hearing shall be tape-recorded upon the request of either party.

1. Upon entering the precinct at 7:00 a.m. after his overnight shift, Officer Hallick is notified verbally that he must appear immediately before a board of captains for an administrative meeting. When Officer Hallick enters the room, the board of captains begin questioning him about his relationship with another officer who is being investigated. After two hours of interrogation without any substantial breaks, Officer Hallick demands that the rest of the session be recorded. One of the captains says, "Sorry, Hallick, that is just not going to happen today."

   According to the sequence of events discussed above, how many of the articles listed in Section 10 of the State Code were violated?

   (A) two
   (B) three
   (C) four
   (D) five

2. Officer Jenson received an official, written notification that she would have to appear before the board of captains for an investigative administrative meeting in fourteen business days. Officer Jenson appeared at the meeting, which took place in the chief's conference room. The board of captains began interrogating Officer Jenson immediately after she entered the room. After the first question, Officer Jenson paused, requesting that the meeting be recorded. The board agreed. The meeting lasted one hour, with two five-minute breaks. An official copy of the tape was placed on record.

   According to the sequence of events discussed above, how many of the articles listed in Section 10 of the State Code were violated?

   (A) none
   (B) one
   (C) two
   (D) three

3. Officer Wilson received an official, written notification that he would have to appear before the board of captains for an investigative administrative meeting in seven business days. Officer Wilson appeared at the meeting, which took place in the chief's conference room. The board of captains began interrogating Officer Wilson immediately after explaining that the meeting would be taped and reading the Statement of Rights. The meeting lasted two hours, with two thirty-minute breaks. An official copy of the tape was placed on record.

   According to the sequence of events discussed above, how many of the articles listed in Section 10 of the State Code were violated?

   (A) none
   (B) one
   (C) two
   (D) three

Questions 4 – 6 refer to the following excerpt.

Section 198-212, The Rules and Regulations of the Metropolitan Police Concerning Disciplinary Action

1. It is mandatory that all disciplinary matters within the agency maintain the rules and regulations established by the merit board in consultation with the chief of police.

2. There are four possible disciplinary actions that can be delivered once an infraction is fully investigated:
   - documented warning
   - suspension (without pay)
   - demotion in merit rank
   - termination and discharge

3. Agency members believed to be in violation of a board-approved rule or regulation can be placed on administrative leave, with pay, for up to forty-five (45) calendar days by the chief of police, pending a thorough internal investigation and determination by the Internal Investigations Department. This initial leave will not be considered a punishment; rather, it will be defined as normal agency procedure.

4. While the Internal Investigations Department will carry out a thorough investigation and offer a determination, the authority to discipline an agency subordinate ultimately rests solely within the power of the chief of police. Following the investigation, the chief can choose to:
   - issue a documented warning, which will be filed for future consideration within an agency member's Human Resources file.
   - suspend the officer, without pay, anywhere from a minimum of seven (7) calendar days to a maximum of three (3) calendar months (whenever an agency member is suspended without pay, they may appeal this disciplinary action within one (1) month of their suspension).
   - demote the agency member and lower their merit rank by no more than one (1) official rank (whenever an agency member is demoted, they may appeal this disciplinary action within one (1) month of their demotion).
   - recommend that the agency member be terminated and discharged from their duties (any recommendation for termination and discharge must first be taken to an administrative hearing).

4. Officer Leon broke one of the agency's rules and regulations, so Chief Armstrong places her on leave with pay for forty-five calendar days. The chief refers the case to a disciplinary board of captains for recommendation. The board recommends suspending the officer for three calendar months. The chief follows this advice, deciding to suspend Officer Leon for three calendar months without pay.

    According to the sequence of events discussed above, what grounds might Officer Leon have for an appeal?

    **(A)** any suspension without pay can be appealed
    **(B)** she was placed on leave without pay
    **(C)** she only broke one rule or regulation
    **(D)** she did not receive a written reprimand

5. Officer Stevens broke one of the department rules and regulations established by the chief, merit board, and Department of Public Safety. Chief Carter places Officer Stevens on leave, without pay, for forty-five calendar days. Unsure of how to handle the matter, the chief refers the case to a disciplinary board of captains for recommendation. The board recommends suspending the officer for nine calendar days. The chief follows this advice, deciding to suspend Officer Stevens for nine calendar days without pay.

According to the sequence of events discussed above, what grounds might Officer Stevens have for an appeal?

- **(A)** the number of days of suspension warrants such an appeal
- **(B)** he should have been placed on leave *with* pay
- **(C)** he only broke one rule or regulation
- **(D)** he did not receive a written reprimand

6. If Officer Leon was notified of a demotion, how many months would she have to appeal?
   - **(A)** one
   - **(B)** three
   - **(C)** nine
   - **(D)** twelve

Questions 7 – 11 refer to the following table.

*The merit board has recently reviewed and revised the Disciplinary Code at the Metropolitan Police Department. The Disciplinary Code now reads as follows:*

Index of Disciplinary Consequences, 2019 – 2020

| | |
|---|---|
| **Written Warning to Suspension** | - Excessive loitering during work hours<br>- Inefficiency or insubordination in the workplace |
| **Written Warning to Discharge** | - Excessive absenteeism or tardiness<br>- Abuse of the Metropolitan Police Department's property, tools, or materials<br>- Conduct that reflects unfavorably on the Metropolitan Police Department<br>- Falsification of records (including material omission of information)<br>- Offensive conduct or language in the workplace<br>- Discriminatory actions<br>- Falsification of time sheets or department reimbursements<br>- Abusing the sick leave policy (or any other related policy)<br>- Harassment in the workplace<br>- Intoxicated while on the job |
| **Suspension to Discharge** | - Refusal to participate in a department-authorized physical examination when asked<br>- Participation in political activities while on duty<br>- Repeated rule violations or infractions<br>- Unauthorized use of weapons |
| **Automatic Discharge** | Membership in an anti-government institution or revolutionary group that threatens to overthrow the US government |
| **Compulsory Resignation** | - Three (3) consecutive absences without administrative approval<br>- Felony offense |

7. Officer Boyer has been loitering in the precinct during work hours, which has reduced his productivity. According to the list above, what is the MOST severe disciplinary action Officer Boyer can receive for his actions?
   (A) written warning
   (B) suspension
   (C) discharge
   (D) compulsory resignation

8. Following an investigation, Officer Hampton is found to be a part of an extremist group that is seeking to overthrow the US government. According to protocol, what is the necessary disciplinary action?
   (A) written warning
   (B) suspension
   (C) automatic discharge
   (D) compulsory resignation

9. Officer Murray is caught accidentally bringing her hunting rifle, an unauthorized firearm, on county property. According to protocol, what is the LEAST severe disciplinary action Officer Murray can receive?
   (A) written warning
   (B) suspension
   (C) discharge
   (D) compulsory resignation

10. Officer Romero did not show up to duty for three days in a row. His leave was not administratively authorized. According to protocol, what is the necessary disciplinary action?
    (A) written warning
    (B) suspension
    (C) discharge
    (D) compulsory resignation

11. Officer Gordon is written up for insubordination. This is his first disciplinary action, as he is usually on good standing with his supervisors. What is the MOST LIKELY disciplinary action?
    (A) written warning
    (B) suspension
    (C) discharge
    (D) compulsory resignation

Questions 12 and 13 refer to the following excerpt on unattended vehicles.

When a police officer arrives at an unattended vehicle during a routine patrol, he or she should adhere to the following protocols:
1. notify radio dispatch about the location and description of vehicle
2. call a tow truck to remove the vehicle, if necessary
3. ask radio dispatch to run the license plate (if there is one on the car) to determine if the car has been reported stolen
4. try to contact the vehicle's owner(s)
5. make a log of all actions and communications in an activity log

**12.** Officer Morrison is on a routine patrol when she observes an abandoned vehicle parked on the side of a highway, presenting a danger to commuters. She communicates the vehicle's location and description to radio dispatch and calls for a tow truck. After running the license plate, radio dispatch reports that the car is not reported stolen. What is Officer Morrison's next step?

   **(A)** report to a ranking officer about the location of the car
   **(B)** contact the vehicle's owner(s)
   **(C)** make a log of all actions and communications in an activity log
   **(D)** make note of the make, model, and color of the vehicle

**13.** Officer McNamara notices an abandoned vehicle in the parking lot of a state park after the park has closed. The car is not obstructing traffic. No rules are posted about vehicle parked after hours. He radios dispatch about the location of the car; provides the make, model, and color of the vehicle; and runs the license plate. Next, he notes all communications in an activity log. According to the protocols above, what step did Officer McNamara forget to take?

   **(A)** call a tow truck
   **(B)** provide a description of the vehicle to radio dispatch
   **(C)** make a note of all actions and communications in an activity log
   **(D)** try to contact the vehicle's owner(s)

Questions 14 and 15 refer to the following excerpt on procedures for intoxicated drivers.

If an officer believes a motorist is driving under the influence of alcohol, the officer should follow these procedures:

1. Issue a separate citation for any original traffic offense (i.e., speeding).
2. Confiscate the driver's license if they take a blood alcohol test and score over the legal limit. The officer also reserves the right to confiscate a driver's license if they refuse to take a blood alcohol test.
3. Do not confiscate the driver's license if the driver takes a blood alcohol test and does NOT exceed the legal limit of intoxication. Officers may still implement field sobriety assessments if they suspect that the driver is intoxicated.
4. Even if a blood alcohol test does not exceed the legal limit, the officer maintains the right to validate a DUI charge if the person fails a set of field sobriety assessments.

**14.** Officer White issues a ticket for reckless driving to a motorist whose car was swerving on the highway. She then asks the driver to take a blood alcohol test. The driver is under the legal limit of alcohol consumption and passes the test. However, Officer White still believes the driver may be intoxicated and under the influence of alcohol.

What is the next appropriate step for Officer White?

   **(A)** make the driver submit to another blood alcohol test
   **(B)** confiscate the driver's license
   **(C)** issue a citation for driving under the influence of alcohol
   **(D)** carry out a field sobriety assessment

**15.** Officer Del Rio pulls over a speeding SUV and issues the driver a speeding ticket. However, he suspects that the driver is intoxicated. He asks the driver to take a blood alcohol test. The driver refuses.

What is the next appropriate step for Officer Del Rio?

   **(A)** confiscate the driver's license
   **(B)** carry out field sobriety assessments
   **(C)** call for backup
   **(D)** make the driver take the blood alcohol test

**Problem Sensitivity**

Officer Singh has been observing the behavior and attitude of Officer Brown, a new police officer. Singh has noticed that Brown is usually calm and happy but sometimes appears to be restless and anxious. At first, Singh thought the mood swings stemmed from issues at home, but then he started to notice Brown's behavior becoming more erratic. Singh asked Brown if everything was okay at home. He noticed Brown's pupils were dilated, his eyes were bloodshot, and his hands were shaking. Brown snapped at Singh, telling him to "leave him alone." Singh saw Brown with what appeared to be pills in a plastic bag in Brown's locker. When Brown saw Singh, he concealed the bag. Later that day, Brown apologized to Singh for being rude. He told Singh that everything was okay at home and not to worry. Singh was not convinced by his statement.

1. What is MOST LIKELY causing Brown's erratic behavior?
   (A) family problems
   (B) financial issues
   (C) drug use
   (D) job stress

2. What is the most suspicious observation made by Officer Singh?
   (A) Brown's mood swings
   (B) Brown's bloodshot eyes
   (C) Brown's apology
   (D) Brown's bag of pills

3. What is the MOST LIKELY reason that Officer Brown apologized to Officer Singh?
   (A) He felt bad for being rude.
   (B) He wanted to put Singh at ease after being caught with pills.
   (C) He got in trouble with a superior officer for his behavior.
   (D) He was encouraged to apologize by his family.

Officer Keating is investigating an attempted robbery near Giant Grocery Store, reported via a 911 call by a store clerk, Kelly Ziccardo. Officer Keating is at the Giant Grocery Store interviewing witnesses. The following information is from witness statements:

Harry Cartwright, the victim of the attempted robbery, states that he was going to Giant Grocery Store to buy a pack of cigarettes when a homeless man accosted him, asking him for money. Cartwright says it was a little after 7:00 p.m. because he remembers hearing the local church bells ringing a few minutes earlier, and they ring every day at that time. When Cartwright refused to give the money, the panhandler, who seemed skittish, tried to threaten him with a knife. Cartwright laughed the situation off, saying, "Oh, you've got to be kidding me." But before he could finish his comment, the man had him pinned to the curb outside the store. Cartwright hit his head on the curb. Around that time, Cartwright saw Jim Lord, a fellow customer, pull out a licensed, concealed firearm. He pointed the gun at the panhandler, shouting, "Drop your weapon!" Kelly Ziccardo emerged from the store, shouting, "I'm calling the police!" That is when Cartwright felt the man release his grip.

John Albright, a twenty-six-year-old customer who was parked in the parking lot at the time of the incident, claims the homeless man had previously solicited him for drugs and money. Albright, who claims to be "street savvy," says the homeless man looked a bit paranoid, asking him for "a fix or some cash." He also says the man's name is Michael Coatesville, and he is known to be a local addict with a history of violence. Albright says he did not see the incident, but he stopped his car when he heard a commotion near the door's entrance.

Kelly Ziccardo, a forty-five-year-old cashier, says she did not see much because everything happened so fast. She says she had just clocked in for her 7:00 p.m. shift when she heard someone shout, "Drop your weapon!" She remembers looking at the cash register, and it said 7:07 p.m. That is when she ran out, shouting, "I'm calling the police!"

Jim Lord, a twenty-three-year-old military veteran, says he was just going to the grocery store after his twelve-hour shift at Reading Anthracite. His shift ended at 6:45 p.m. and it usually took him around twenty minutes to get to the store. He remembers pulling up to the store at 7:05 p.m. He claims he was just grabbing a shopping cart when he saw a homeless man draw his knife on another man. He says he was trained in the military to handle these situations, and he felt the man was enough of a threat to draw his licensed firearm. He says he was "just trying to be a good citizen," and he did not get a good look at the man's face, but he definitely scared him off.

4. What time did Jim Lord MOST LIKELY try to intervene in the robbery?
   (A) 6:45 p.m.
   (B) 7:00 p.m.
   (C) 7:05 p.m.
   (D) 7:07 p.m.

5. According to the testimonies taken, what was likely the intent of the attempted robbery?
   (A) to get money for drugs
   (B) to rob the cash register
   (C) to get money for food
   (D) to buy a pack of cigarettes

6. Which witness is MOST LIKELY to provide the most reliable details about the crime?
   (A) Officer Keating
   (B) Kelly Zicchardo
   (C) John Albright
   (D) Jim Lord

Officer Crawley must respond to a prowler call at Sixteenth and Center Streets. He is the first officer to arrive at the scene and waits for backup in his patrol car. A civilian approaches the officer. The civilian matches the description of the suspected prowler. The civilian complains that the patrol car is in his neighborhood, taking up perfectly good parking spaces. He asks Officer Crawley what the problem is and offers to help search the neighborhood for any suspicious activity because he is part of the Neighborhood Watch program.

7. Which of the following is the MOST appropriate action for Officer Crawley to take in this situation?
   (A) send the civilian on a quick mission to search the vicinity and, if necessary, join the search
   (B) arrest the civilian immediately for prowling
   (C) radio for immediate backup just in case the civilian is the actual prowler
   (D) engage the civilian in conversation to decide whether he is the suspect

The following are the statements of witnesses concerning four different arson incidents.

**Witness 1**: Jack Cho was on his way to work when he noticed a young man running away from a building. A moment later, he noticed the building was in flames. The young man was tall and very thin.

**Witness 2**: Kirk Browning was drinking coffee in his kitchen when he looked out the window and saw the house across the street on fire. He ran to the back door. When he looked out from his back door, he saw a group of teenagers running away from the building.

**Witness 3**: Troy Saunders was working outside when he saw flames coming from an office window. He then saw a man in his forties quickly driving away in his car.

**Witness 4**: Arnie Haynes was going to the local bar when he heard a man screaming that his house was on fire. He noticed a tall, young man running away from the scene.

8. Which two witnesses MOST LIKELY saw the same arsonist, according to the information above?
    (A) Jack Cho and Troy Saunders
    (B) Kirk Browning and Troy Saunders
    (C) Jack Cho and Arnie Haynes
    (D) Kirk Browning and Arnie Haynes

Officer Gordon responds to an incident at Mrs. Pilconis's home. She tells him that her black 2019 Ford Expedition has been stolen, claiming that the last time she saw it was when she parked it across the street from her house at 2:00 a.m. After completing the interview, Officer Gordon returns to his squad car to prepare his report, in which he writes that Mrs. Pilconis reported that her black SUV was stolen. He also writes that the vehicle was last seen at 2:00 a.m. across the street from her house where she parked it.

9. What did Officer Gordon forget to report?
    (A) the time the vehicle was last seen
    (B) the last known location of the vehicle
    (C) the color of the vehicle
    (D) the make and model of the vehicle

Officer Brenner is conducting a routine patrol of a neighborhood where a string of burglaries has recently taken place. She notices that a suspicious-looking man wearing dark clothing matches the description of the man reported to be involved in the burglaries. The man is moving quickly past her patrol car, refusing to make eye contact and staring at the ground.

10. What should Officer Brenner do?
    (A) draw her weapon and tell the man to lie on the ground
    (B) interview neighbors for their testimonies
    (C) continue her routine patrol of the neighborhood
    (D) stop the man and ask him what is going on

A fellow officer regularly gets into irrational arguments with citizens while on patrol. Most of the time the incidents are minor and no one notices. However, at other times, his behavior reflects poorly on the department. After witnessing a particularly troubling situation, his partner feels like something must be said about the officer's behavior.

11. How should the partner handle the situation?
    (A) apologize to citizens when he berates them in public
    (B) speak to the commanding officer, since it is not his duty to discipline the officer
    (C) speak to the officer in private to explain the consequences of his behavior
    (D) ignore the behavior since, as his peer, there is nothing he can do

Officer Bailey interviewed four witnesses to a bank robbery. Each one described the suspects as follows:

**Witness 1**: "Both men had on gray slacks, black dress shoes, and suit coats. One coat was gray, the other was black. One of the men had long blond hair. The other man's hair was not visible because he had a

Halloween mask on. They both looked short—less than six feet tall. The man with the mask was the only one who spoke."

**Witness 2**: "Both of the men were about the same size. They were short—certainly less than six feet tall, and neither could've weighed more than 175 pounds. One of them was wearing a black suit coat, and the other one was wearing a gray suit coat. I couldn't see their faces. One had a Halloween mask on. The other one, the one with long blond hair, was wearing a green bandana over his face."

**Witness 3**: "Both of the men were tall. Both had suit coats on. They were also wearing blue jeans and tennis shoes. One had blond hair with a bandana. The other one was wearing some kind of mask. Neither of them spoke."

**Witness 4**: "There were two people involved. Both were men. They were short for men. Less than six feet tall. They had slim builds. One of them had long blond hair. He was wearing a green bandana, gray slacks, and a gray suit coat. The other had a black suit coat. He was wearing a Halloween mask, so I could not see his hair. Only the one with the Halloween mask spoke. His voice sounded muffled, but he sounded like he had an accent."

12. Which witness's testimony is MOST LIKELY flawed?
    - (A) Witness 1
    - (B) Witness 2
    - (C) Witness 3
    - (D) Witness 4

You and your partner respond to a domestic assault incident involving a male suspect. When the suspect is detained, he kicks your partner. Your partner spits on the suspect while in custody.

13. What is the MOST appropriate way to handle this situation?
    - (A) report the incident to his supervisor without an initial conversation
    - (B) tell your partner that his behavior was inappropriate and remind him that if it happens again it must be reported
    - (C) tell the officer that his behavior was inappropriate and that he needs to tell his supervisor or else you will have to report it
    - (D) ignore the incident because the spitting was reactionary to the suspect's violent behavior

You and your partner arrive at a house where a burglary is reported to be occurring. As you approach the house you hear a woman scream in the backyard. The gate is open. You hear a man yell, "Shut up or I'll kill you!" You also hear a warning shot fired in the air. Your partner is visibly anxious and asks, "What should we do?"

14. What is the MOST appropriate way to handle this situation?
    - (A) radio dispatch to see if it is the correct house before acting
    - (B) tell your partner to stay in the car so you can knock on the door
    - (C) try to enter the backyard and contact a supervisor after the situation is under control
    - (D) wait for your supervisor's permission to enter the building

You are patrolling a neighborhood with your partner in a patrol car. He initiates a traffic stop on a sedan with a broken taillight. The driver of the sedan refuses to stop and speeds away from the patrol car. You radio dispatch to inform your team that you are pursuing a vehicle that disregarded a routine traffic stop and is now speeding. Your shift supervisor instructs you to cancel the pursuit.

**15.** What is the MOST appropriate way to handle this situation?
- **A)** confirm that you understand the order and stop following the sedan
- **B)** ignore your supervisor's order and continue following the sedan
- **C)** radio another police officer to continue the pursuit on your behalf
- **D)** radio your supervisor to cancel the order and continue the pursuit

## Spatial Orientation

Refer to the following maps to answer the questions.

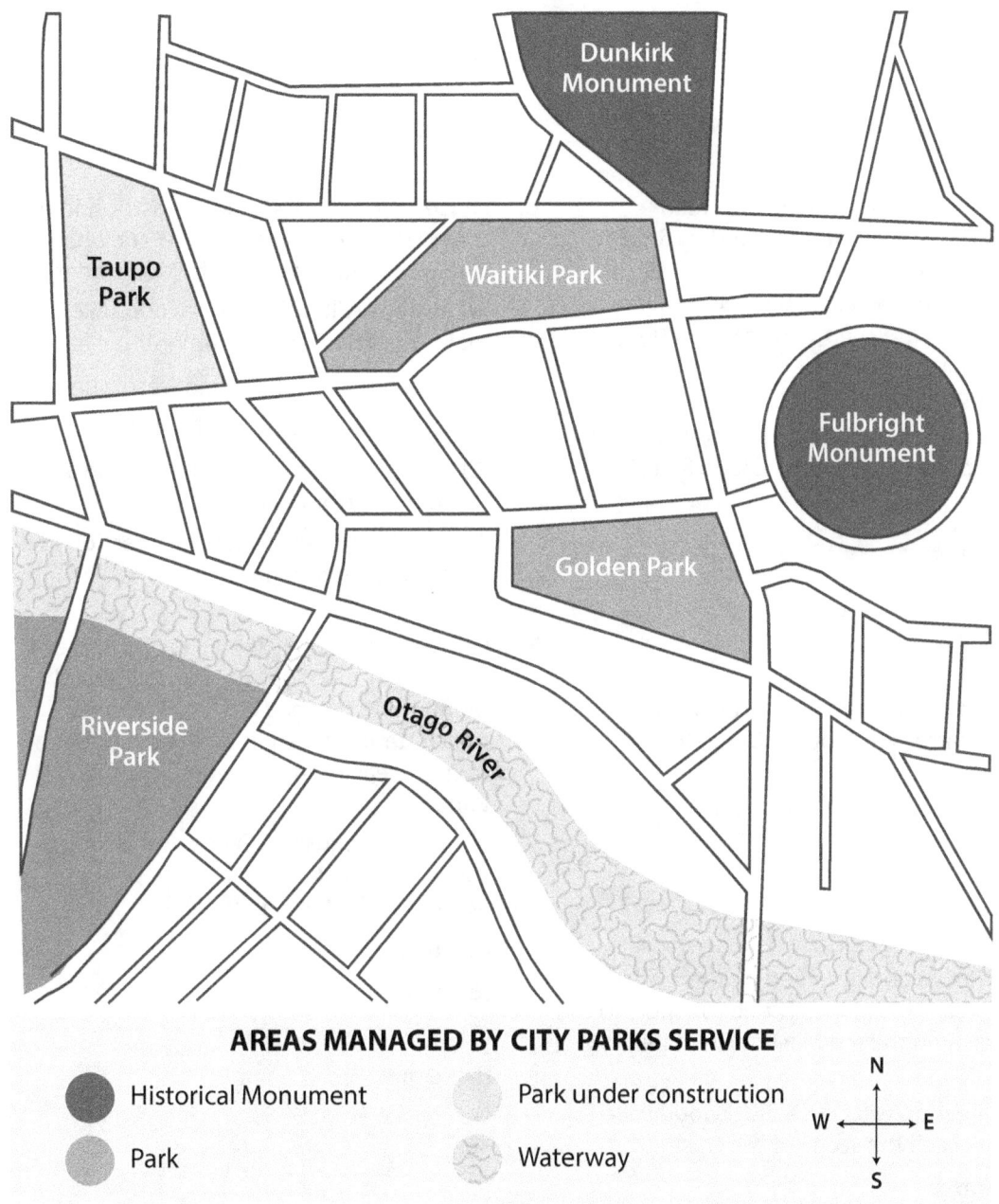

The previous map depicts the entire area of Officer Rockwood's patrol jurisdiction.

1. Officer Rockwood is heading north, rounding the circular drive that surrounds the Fulbright Monument on its east side, when he gets a call to report to the east side of Waitiki Park for an alleged armed robbery.

   How many right-hand turns will Officer Rockwood make to reach the park?

   (A) one
   (B) two
   (C) three
   (D) four

2. Officer Rockwood is parked on a road that serves as the eastern boundary for Riverside Park when he is told to patrol all parks near him because the precinct just got an anonymous tip that a large drug deal is happening at one of the parks in his jurisdiction.

   How many parks will Officer Rockwood need to patrol north of the Otago River?

   (A) one
   (B) three
   (C) four
   (D) five

3. How many parks will Officer Rockwood need to patrol south of the Otago River?

   (A) one
   (B) three
   (C) four
   (D) five

4. Officer Rockwood is parked on the road just north of Waitiki Park. He is told to report to a car crash on the road just north of Taupo Park.

   What direction will Officer Rockwood have to go to reach the scene of the crash?

   (A) north
   (B) south
   (C) east
   (D) west

5. Officer Rockwood is moving southbound on the road just east of Waitiki Park. He is asked to take the fastest route to the nearest intersection of a road and the Otago River.

   How many four-way intersections will Officer Rockwood encounter on his journey?

   (A) three
   (B) four
   (C) five
   (D) six

6. Officer Rockwood is headed eastbound on the road just north of Golden Park when he is told to report to Fulbright Monument.

   What steps will Officer Rockwood take to make it to Fulbright Monument?

   (A) make a U-turn and head westbound
   (B) continue heading eastbound
   (C) take a left at the next intersection and head northbound
   (D) take a right at the next intersection and head southbound

7. Officer Rockwood just made a right to exit the circular road that surrounds Fulbright Monument. He needs to return to the police station, which is across the street from the easternmost boundary of Taupo Park.

   How many roads will Officer Rockwood travel on to make it back to the police station by the fastest route?

   (A) two
   (B) four
   (C) six
   (D) eight

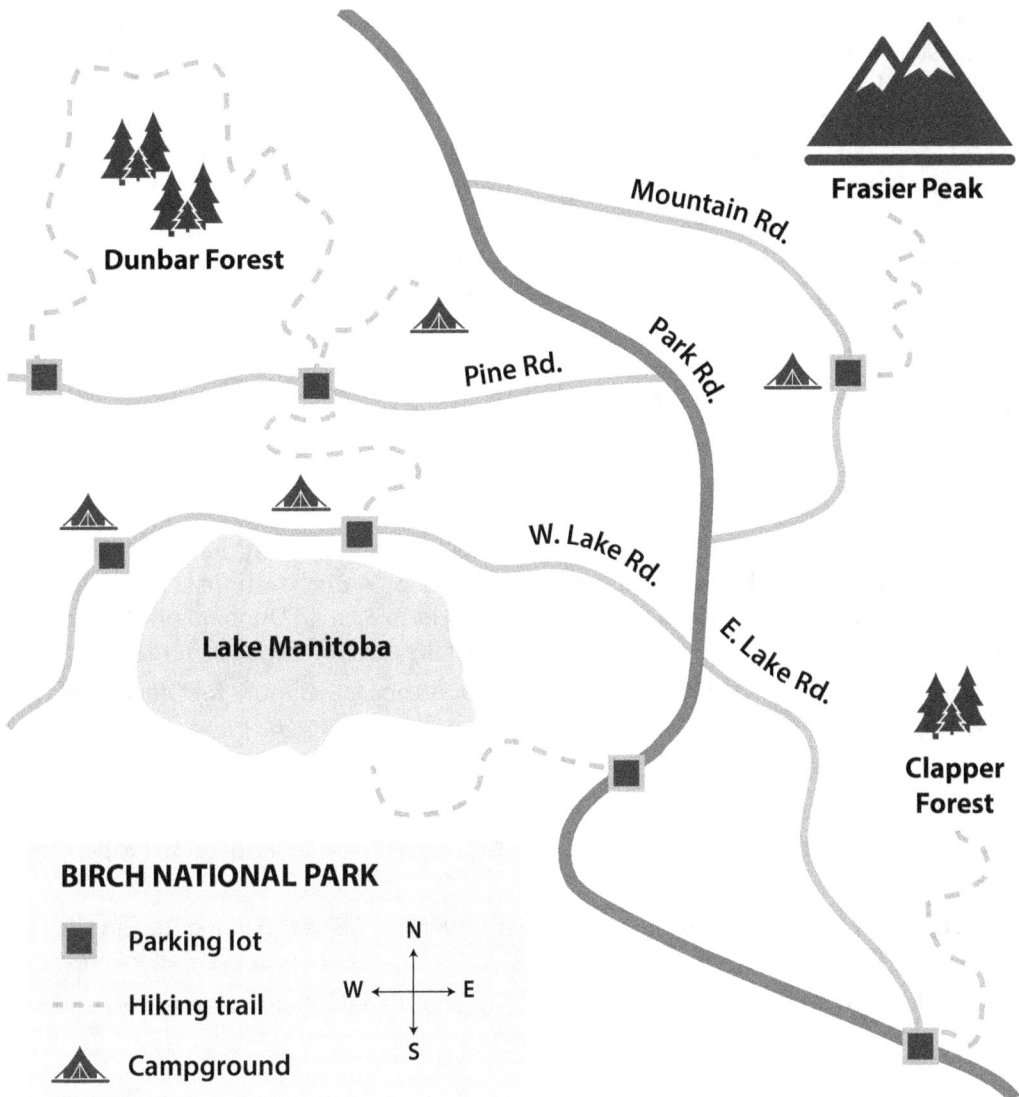

8. Officer Rue just passed the intersection of Park Road and E. Lake Road, heading northbound on Park Road. He is radioed to respond to an arson incident at the small visitor's center located at the trailhead of Frasier Peak.

   What route will Officer Rue take to respond to this incident?

   (A) make a left on W. Lake Road
   (B) make a right on Mountain Road
   (C) make a left on Pine Road
   (D) stay northbound on Park Road

9. A family is reported missing near Lake Manitoba. How many campgrounds will Officer Rue have to search?

   (A) one
   (B) two
   (C) three
   (D) four

10. Officer Rue is on foot patrol for the day. He is currently located on Park Road, just north of the intersection of Park Road and Mountain Road, just north of the intersection with W. and E. Lake Road. He has to respond on foot to the trailhead that leads to Clapper Forest. While on foot, Officer Rue, who is familiar with the landscape, is allowed to walk on land not designated as roads or trails.

    If Officer Rue travels in a straight line from his current location to the trailhead to Clapper Forest, what direction will he travel?

    (A) southwest
    (B) southeast
    (C) northwest
    (D) northeast

11. Officer Rue is parked at the parking lot on Pine Road closest to the trail that connects Pine Road with W. Lake Road. He is told to drive to the parking lot on W. Lake Road that is closest to the trail that connects Pine Road with W. Lake Road.

    What roads will Officer Rue drive on to reach his destination?

    (A) Pine Road and W. Lake Road
    (B) Pine Road and Mountain Road
    (C) Pine Road, Park Road, and E. Lake Road
    (D) Pine Road, Park Road, and W. Lake Road

12. Officer Rue has parked his patrol car near the westernmost campground in the park. He receives orders to report to the trailhead that leads to the campground just south of Lake Manitoba.

    What route will Officer Rue have to follow to reach this campground?

    (A) west on W. Lake Road and south on Park Road
    (B) west on W. Lake Road and north on Park Road
    (C) east on W. Lake Road and south on Park Road
    (D) east on W. Lake Road and north on Park Road

13. What direction will Officer Rue travel to reach the southernmost campground in the park?

    (A) south
    (B) southeast
    (C) west
    (D) southwest

14. Officer Rue is on foot patrol for the day. He is currently located at the trailhead for Frasier Peak. While on foot, Officer Rue, who is familiar with the landscape, is allowed to walk on land not designated as roads or trails.

    What direction will Officer Rue travel to reach the easternmost campground in the park?

    (A) north
    (B) south
    (C) east
    (D) west

15. Officer Rue is parked at the westernmost parking lot in Birch National Park. He has to respond to a fire in Dunbar Forest. He can only take designated trails or roads.

    What is the fastest route for Officer Rue to reach Dunbar Forest?

    (A) east to the next parking lot and then take the trail north to Dunbar Forest
    (B) north on the trail closest to his parking lot
    (C) west to the next parking lot and then take the trail north to Dunbar Forest
    (D) south on the trail closest to his parking lot

## Information Ordering

Analyze the list of information points. Then, determine the logical order in which they should fall.

Officer Bailey responds to a recent assault on the boardwalk in Atlantic City, New Jersey. He receives the following testimony from the victim:

1. I bought some cotton candy right by the boardwalk and began taking a peaceful stroll.
2. I just got off my shift at the local restaurant when I decided to buy some cotton candy and go for a walk on the boardwalk.
3. He asked for some money.

4. A vagrant—he was about five foot six, frail, shirtless, and with a gray beard—approached me about thirty minutes into my walk.
5. I refused to give him any money.
6. When I refused his request, he grabbed me by the throat before a Good Samaritan scared him off.

1. What is the MOST logical order for the steps listed above?
   (A) 2, 1, 4, 3, 5, 6
   (B) 1, 6, 3, 5, 4, 2
   (C) 2, 1, 5, 6, 3, 4
   (D) 1, 2, 6, 5, 3, 4

Officer Morales just interviewed the victim of an assault and robbery. The following statements appeared in the victim's testimony about the incident:

1. I ran into my backyard after breaking free from his grip.
2. He grabbed my arm, but I escaped.
3. I rounded the corner of William Cannon and Salt Springs Drive near my home.
4. As I rounded the corner, I saw Daniel Davidson, my brother's friend.
5. I did not want to interact with Daniel because he looked like he was "speeding" on narcotics.
6. He snatched my purse while I was on the ground and I began to cry.
7. A neighbor heard me crying.
8. Daniel chased me into my backyard and tackled me to the ground.
9. The neighbor chased Daniel away.
10. Daniel refused to let me pass even though I was ignoring him.

2. What is the most logical order for the FIRST five events in this testimony?
   (A) 4, 1, 2, 10, 6
   (B) 3, 4, 5, 10, 2
   (C) 5, 3, 4, 9, 7
   (D) 2, 8, 6, 7, 9

3. What is the most logical order of the SECOND five events in this testimony?
   (A) 1, 8, 6, 7, 9
   (B) 2, 8, 6, 7, 9
   (C) 3, 4, 5, 10, 2
   (D) 10, 2, 3, 5, 9

When transporting a person placed under arrest, these protocols should be followed (note: these protocols are not listed in the correct order):

1. handcuff the person
2. place the person in the back of the police cruiser
3. notify radio dispatch of the arrest
4. carry out a wingspan search for weapons, narcotics, or other illicit items

4. What is the MOST logical order for the protocols above?
   (A) 4, 1, 2, 3
   (B) 1, 3, 2, 4
   (C) 2, 4, 3, 1
   (D) 3, 1, 2, 4

A police officer goes to a local gas station to gather information about a recent crime. The following details were taken from witness testimonies:

1. The two men escaped through a side door just after the police told them to stop.
2. One of the men pointed a gun at me, and ordered that I hand over the cash from the cash register.
3. The police came into the gas station and attempted to deter the two men from escaping.
4. Two masked men entered the gas station.
5. I handed over the cash just as the police made it to the scene.

5. What is the MOST logical order for the events described above?
   (A) 1, 3, 2, 4, 5
   (B) 4, 2, 5, 3, 1
   (C) 2, 3, 4, 1, 5
   (D) 2, 4, 5, 3, 1

A police officer reports to the scene of a recent stabbing. The witnesses give the following details in their testimonies:

1. The woman's brother, the owner of the bar, monitored it for a bit, and stepped outside with a sharp object in his hand that looked like a tool or ice pick "when he could not take it anymore."
2. A man and a woman were arguing outside a bar.
3. The brother threatened to stab the man.
4. He jabbed a sharp object into the man's abdomen.
5. They were arguing so forcefully that it got the attention of everyone in the bar, including the woman's brother, the owner of the bar.

6. What is the MOST logical order for the events described above?
   (A) 5, 2, 3, 1, 4
   (B) 4, 3, 2, 1, 5
   (C) 2, 5, 1, 3, 4
   (D) 2, 1, 5, 3, 4

A police officer arrives at the scene of a car burglary. The officer receives the following details from a local resident:

1. I saw an old man park his car and go into the school.
2. The old man came out of the school when he heard the window breaking.
3. He used the tool to break the window.
4. As soon as he walked through the door, a young man wearing a red hooded sweatshirt turned the corner and approached the car with a tool in his hand.
5. He yelled at the young man for breaking into his car, and the young man ran down Eleventh Street with an iPhone in his hand.

7. What is the MOST logical order for the events described above?
   (A) 1, 2, 3, 4, 5
   (B) 1, 4, 5, 2, 3
   (C) 1, 4, 3, 2, 5
   (D) 5, 1, 2, 3, 4

Police officers must not only stop crime; they must also know how to treat those who are critically injured at crime scenes. Some injuries a police officer might encounter include:

1. shock
2. heart failure
3. deep wound bleeding
4. non-protruding broken bone
5. minor lacerations

8. A victim of a crime is affected by all of these injuries, and an ambulance has not yet arrived. In what order should a police officer treat these injuries?
    (A) 2, 3, 1, 4, 5
    (B) 5, 4, 1, 3, 2
    (C) 4, 5, 1, 2, 3
    (D) 5, 3, 2, 1, 4

A police officer arrives at the scene of an arson incident. While interviewing several witnesses to the crime, the officer receives the following statements:

1. Sandy Gomez saw two teenagers running with some fireworks toward an alleyway.
2. The teenagers ignored her question and ran into the alleyway.
3. She yelled at the teenagers, "Hey, where are you going?" immediately after she saw them running toward the alleyway.
4. About two minutes later, she heard glass breaking and a big booming sound.
5. Seconds after she heard these sounds, she noticed the smoke and flames coming from a garage in the alleyway.
6. She saw the teens run off from the smoke and flames, and that is when she called 911.

9. What is the MOST logical order for the events described above?
    (A) 1, 3, 2, 4, 5, 6
    (B) 5, 1, 3, 2, 4, 6
    (C) 1, 2, 3, 4, 5, 6
    (D) 5, 4, 6, 2, 3, 1

Officer Atkins, a police officer at the University of Richmond, arrives at the scene of a vandalism attempt. Atkins receives the following testimonies from witnesses:

1. We showed up late to the protest. By the time we got there, it was already pretty out of control. From far away, we could see the flames of a bonfire that had been started near the controversial statue on campus.
2. The police arrived just as the first statue tumbled to the ground. The protesters scattered.
3. Before you knew it, the fire was reaching twenty feet in height, and the statue was starting to collapse from the impact.
4. As we got closer to the fire, we noticed three masked protesters damaging not only the controversial statue in the park but other statues as well. They were using sledgehammers to break the concrete foundations.

10. What is the MOST logical order for the events described previously?
    - (A) 1, 2, 3, 4
    - (B) 2, 4, 3, 1
    - (C) 1, 4, 3, 2
    - (D) 3, 4, 1, 2

11. What is the MOST LIKELY reason that the protesters scattered?
    - (A) The fire got out of control.
    - (B) The statue began to collapse.
    - (C) The police arrived.
    - (D) The protest was over.

Officer Garrison is interviewing Betty Stonelake about an armed robbery she witnessed at a local convenience store. The following statements appear in her testimony:

1. I went to the back of the store to pick up a half gallon of milk.
2. That's when I saw the man pull a gun on the cashier and ask for money.
3. I dropped quietly to the ground and waited until I heard the man leave. I knew he was gone because I heard the bells on the door.
4. On my way to the cash register to pay for the milk, I noticed a suspicious man walk into the store.
5. I entered the store at about 3:00 a.m.

12. What is the MOST logical order for the events described above?
    - (A) 1, 5, 4, 2, 3
    - (B) 4, 2, 3, 1, 5
    - (C) 5, 1, 4, 2, 3
    - (D) 1, 4, 2, 3, 5

Detective Harper is interviewing Tara Schmidt, a bartender at a local bar. Ms. Schmidt says that she witnessed an assault on a patron named Bruce Houser. The following statements appear in her testimony:

1. I know that one of the men was Bruce Houser, but I do not know the name of the other man. I noticed them arguing for a bit before I saw the other man push Bruce.
2. I was about midway through my shift when I noticed two men arguing near the restroom.
3. The man exited the side door after the assault.
4. I called the police when the man left because Bruce looked unconscious.
5. At that point, Bruce fell and hit his head on the radiator.

13. What is the MOST logical order for the events described above?
    - (A) 3, 2, 1, 4, 5
    - (B) 1, 2, 5, 3, 4
    - (C) 2, 1, 5, 3, 4
    - (D) 2, 1, 5, 4, 3

You are at a local outdoor shooting range to test your new firearm. As you enter the shooting range, you must review a checklist of the facility's procedures and expectations, which follow (not in order):

1. Facility-approved ear protection must be acquired at the front desk and worn before entering the firing zone.
2. Reloading of any firearm should be done outside of the firing area.
3. Return all ear protection equipment to the front desk before leaving.
4. Firearms must be registered and placed on safety before they can be brought into the facility.
5. Firearms must once again be placed on safety after completion of firing practice.
6. Firearms can be taken off safety immediately prior to firing, once the officer reaches their specific firing area. The officer can proceed to fire at this time.

**14.** What is the MOST logical order for this checklist?
- (A) 4, 1, 6, 2, 5, 3
- (B) 3, 1, 2, 5, 4, 6
- (C) 6, 1, 4, 3, 2, 5
- (D) 5, 3, 2, 1, 6, 4

You went to a local fast-food restaurant to gather information about a crime. The following statements were taken from a witness about an attempted robbery:

1. I was ordered to give the masked woman my jewelry and purse.
2. Two masked men and one masked woman entered the fast-food restaurant.
3. I remained on the scene to provide law enforcement with my statement.
4. I handed my earrings, wedding ring, and purse to the masked woman.
5. The three masked individuals fled through the side door when the first responding police officer arrived.

**15.** What is the MOST logical order for the events described above?
- (A) 1, 2, 3, 5, 4
- (B) 4, 2, 3, 5, 1
- (C) 2, 3, 4, 5, 1
- (D) 2, 1, 4, 5, 3

**Memorization**

Study each image for up to two minutes. Then, answer the questions without referring to the image.

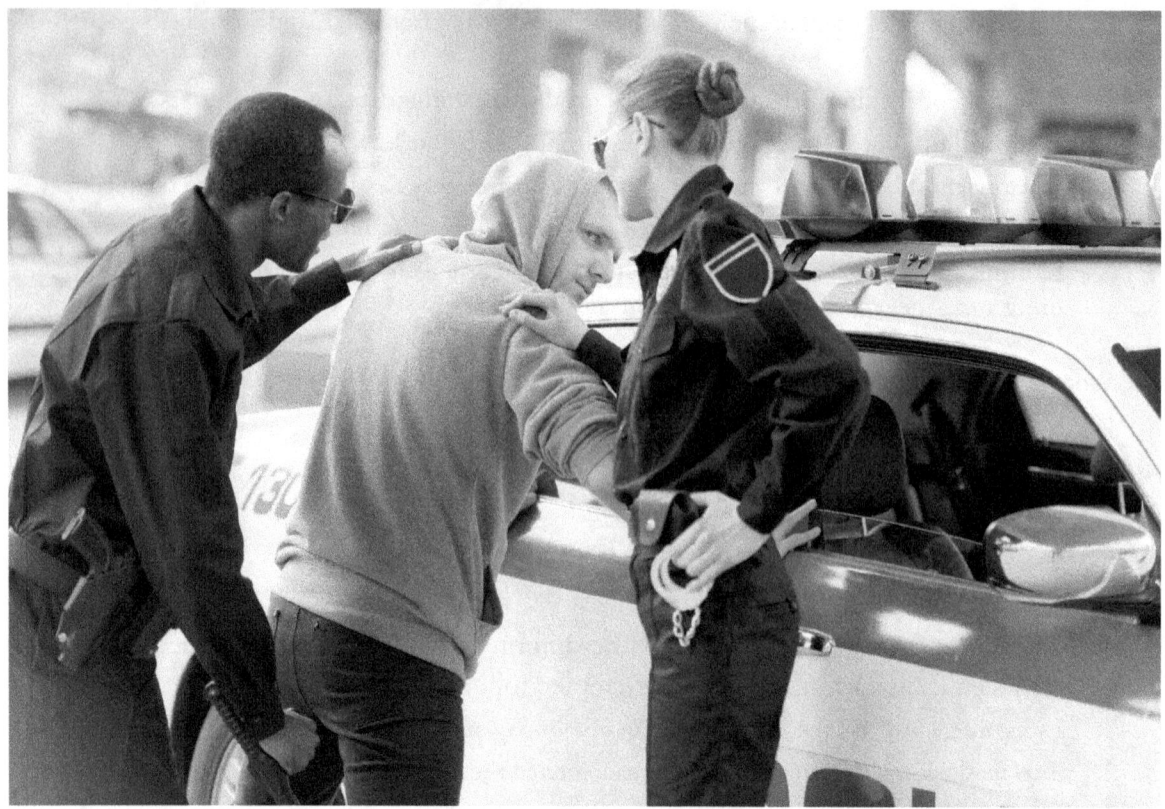

1. What is the suspect in the photograph wearing?

    **(A)** a costume

    **(B)** jeans and a hooded sweatshirt

    **(C)** a jumpsuit

    **(D)** shorts and T-shirt

2. What is the subject leaning against in the photograph?

    **(A)** a wall

    **(B)** a pillar

    **(C)** a fence

    **(D)** a squad car

3. What is the female police officer gripping with her left hand in the photograph?

    **(A)** the suspect

    **(B)** the other police officer's shoulder

    **(C)** handcuffs

    **(D)** the squad car

4. What is pictured in the upper-left-hand corner of the photograph?

   **(A)** a hubcap
   **(B)** broken glass
   **(C)** caution tape
   **(D)** a person on the ground

5. What number is the officer placing near the crime scene?

   **(A)** 1
   **(B)** 2
   **(C)** 3
   **(D)** 4

6. How many people are pictured in the photograph?

   **(A)** one
   **(B)** two
   **(C)** three
   **(D)** four

PRACTICE TEST 111

7. What is the person in the photograph gripping in their right hand?

   (A) a gun
   (B) a magnifying glass
   (C) a brush
   (D) a cell phone

8. How many markers are visible on the ground in the photograph?

   (A) one
   (B) two
   (C) three
   (D) four

9. What is the presumed location of the crime scene?

   (A) a paved city parking lot
   (B) a police station
   (C) a wooded area
   (D) a playground

**10.** What is the police officer on the left MOST LIKELY doing in the photograph?

   **(A)** questioning a suspect
   **(B)** frisking a suspect
   **(C)** detaining a suspect
   **(D)** directing traffic

**11.** What is the suspect in the photograph kneeling next to?

   **(A)** a squad car
   **(B)** another suspect
   **(C)** a traffic cone
   **(D)** a fence

**12.** Which way is the suspect's head facing in the photograph?

   **(A)** to the right
   **(B)** to the left
   **(C)** away from the camera
   **(D)** toward the camera

13. What does it say on the officer's vest in the photograph?
    (A) EVENTS
    (B) POLICE
    (C) LAPD
    (D) NYPD

14. Which direction is the closest car driving in the photograph?
    (A) from right to left
    (B) from left to right
    (C) toward the camera
    (D) away from the camera

15. What is the police officer MOST LIKELY doing in the photograph?
    (A) detaining a suspect
    (B) patrolling in a squad car
    (C) directing traffic and pedestrian crossings
    (D) securing a crime scene

## Visualization

Each of these two images was created using several smaller shapes. Choose the letter corresponding to the piece that was NOT used to create the shape.

1.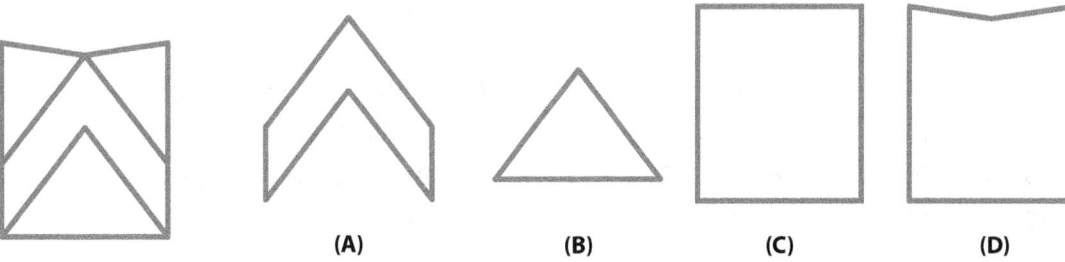

2.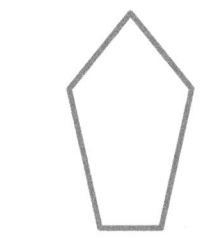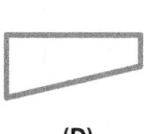

(A)  (B)  (C)  (D)

## Selective Attention

Choose the option that contains the EXACT pattern of symbols, letters, numbers, and spaces.

1. DyYLV5ScQ%=\\ /48X!! hE$ÆQ
   (A) DyYLV5ScQ%=\\ /48X!!! E$ÆQ
   (B) DyYLV5ScQ%=\\ /48X!! hE$ÆQ
   (C) DyYLV5ScQ%=\\ ]48X!! hE$ÆQ
   (D) DYYLV5ScQ%=\\ /48X!! hE$ÆQ

2. @##^790WWX ))(( @!!HVX%=
   (A) @##^790WWX ))(( @!!HVX%=
   (B) @#@^790WWX ))(( @!!HVX%=
   (C) @##^790WWX )))( @!!HVX%=
   (D) @##^790WWX ))(( @!!HVX+=

3. ÆQ** ÆQ** ÆQ++00)((#234
   (A) ÆQ** ÆQ** ÆQ++00)0(#234
   (B) ÆQ**ÆQ**ÆQ++00)((234
   (C) ÆQ** ÆQ** ÆQ++00)((#234
   (D) AE ÆQ** ÆQ++00)((#234

4. {||}[|]**($%& 9 _ ##
   (A) [||]{|}**($%& 9 _ ##
   (B) **($%& 9 _ ##{||}[|]
   (C) [||]{|}**($&% 9 _ ##
   (D) {||}[|]**($%& 9 _ ##

5. ABC*DEF -- &¬£%$^3$T^¥
   (A) ABCD*DEF -- &¬£%$^3$T^¥
   (B) ABC*DEF -- &¬£%$^3$T^¥
   (C) AB*CDEF -- &¬£%$^3$T^¥
   (D) ABC*DEF = &¬£%$^3$T^¥

6. X%$^3$ (;±¬£T**++--= /\
   (A) X%$^3$ (;±¬£T**++--= /\
   (B) X%$^3$ (;±¬£T**++- = /\
   (C) X%$^3$ (;±¬£T**++--= \/
   (D) X%$^3$ (;±¬£T**+=--= /\

7. &DF--=+":"+=--FD&
   (A) &DF--=+':"+=--FD&
   (B) &DF--=+"::"+=--DF&
   (C) &DF--=+"::"+=--FD&
   (D) &DF--+="::"=+--FD&

8. <...>{}\|/ **& **) 09H---{K}{L}[D]
   (A) <..>{}\|/ **& **) 09H---{K}{L}[D]
   (B) <...>{}\|/ **& **) 09H---{K}{L}[D]
   (C) <...>{}\|/ **& **) 09H---{L}{L}[D]
   (D) <...>{}\|/ **& **) 09H---{K}{L}[D]

9. #^#=+=^++^5678 ..9 ^++^ %\
   (A) #^#=+=^++^5678 .9 ^++^ %\
   (B) #^=#+=^++^5678 ..9 ^++^ %\
   (C) #^#=+=^++^5678 ..9 ^++^ %/
   (D) #^#=+=^++^5678 ..9 ^++^ %\

10. }}}o{{{ **%$%** }}}0{{{ <>!<>#3
    (A) }}}o{{{ **%$%** }}}0{{{ <>|<>#3
    (B) }}}0{{{ **%$%** }}}0{{{ <>!<>#3
    (C) }}}o{{{ **%*$%** }}}0{{{ <>!<>#3
    (D) }}}o{{{ **%$%** }}}0{{{ <>!<>#3

11. *$^{3333}$*VVV$^{333}$*9(0)@~_-_RACING`
    (A) *$^{3333}$*VVV$^{333}$*9(0)@~_-_RACING
    (B) *$^{3333}$*VVV$^{333}$*9(0)@~_-_RACING`
    (C) *$^{333}$*VVV$^{3333}$*9(0)@~_-_RACING`
    (D) *$^{3333}$*V^V$^{333}$*9(0)@~_-_RACING`

12. APB:9669!! \|\<^V^>/?\+
    (A) APB:9969!! \|\<^V^>/?\+
    (B) ABB;9669!! \|\<^V^>/?\+
    (C) APB;9969!! \|\<^V^>/?\+
    (D) APB:9669!! \|\<^V^>/?\+

13. 3#8&(5%j&b$ Hgf6:[>?!%
    (A) 3#8&(5%j&b$Hgf6:[>?!%
    (B) 3#8&(5%j&b$ Hgf6:[>?!%
    (C) 3#8$(5%j&b$ Hgf6:[>?!%
    (D) 3#8&(5%j$b$ Hgf6:[>!!%

14. &&^^**(())879-(0)--+ K
    (A) &&^^**( )879-(0)--+K
    (B) &$^^**(())879-(0)--+ K
    (C) &&^^**(())879-(0)--+ K
    (D) &&^^**(0)879-(0)--+ K

15. 8989989998988898899989
    (A) 9898988898999989988898
    (B) 8989989998988898899988
    (C) 8989989998988898899989
    (D) 9988989998988898899989

## Flexibility of Closure

### Box One

```
I?BMBTIOPRDFQSDRABCQSDJAOGQJILOPBMJ?
F?YTREDCMJALAUB?GYFGTEDCFBMAIUWQASXC
GJQJILOPBMJ?F?UJA?TRFDEDSQYTREDCMJALA
UBTIOPRDFQSDRBJIQBJUOLPRTOAECFG?UJAIL
PQTGJIALBBFDABCQSDJAOGCBPLTG?UJAI?BM
BTIOPRDFQSDRABCQSDJAOGCBDRBJIQBJUOLP
RTOAECFG?UJAILPQTGJIALBBFDABCQSDJAOGC
IALBBFDABCQSDJAOGC RTOAECFG?UJAILABAB
```

1. How many question marks (?) appear in the box?
   - (A) 9
   - (B) 10
   - (C) 11
   - (D) 12

2. How many A's appear in the box?
   - (A) 30
   - (B) 29
   - (C) 28
   - (D) 27

3. How many C's appear in the box?
   - (A) 14
   - (B) 15
   - (C) 16
   - (D) 17

### Box Two

```
IOBMBTIOPR!FQS!RXBXQS!ZXOGQZILOPBMZOF
OYTRE!XMZXLXUBOGYFGTE!XFBMXIUWQXSXXG
ZQZRBZIQBZUOLPRTOXEX7GOUZXILPQTGZIXL
BBF!XBXQS!ZXOGX IXLBBF!XBXQS!ZXOGX RTOX
EXFGOUZXILXBXBILOPBMZOFOUZXOTRF!E!SQY
TRE!XMZXLXUBTIOPR!FQS!RBZIQBZXOLPRTOX
EXFGOUZXILPQTGZIXLBBFTXBXQSTZXOGXBPL
TGOUZXIOBMBTIOPR!FQS!RXBXQS!XBTG! XXXX
```

4. How many exclamation points (!) appear in the box?
   - (A) 12
   - (B) 14
   - (C) 16
   - (D) 18

5. How many X's appear in the box?
   - (A) 25
   - (B) 30
   - (C) 50
   - (D) 55

6. How many 7's appear in the box?
   - (A) 0
   - (B) 1
   - (C) 2
   - (D) 3

## Box Three

```
I4BMBTI4PR!FQS!R7B7QS!0742Q0IL4PBM04F4
YTRE!7M07L7UB42YF2TE!7FBM7IUWQ7S7720Q
0RB0IQB0U4LPRT47E7F24U07ILPQT20I7L04F
4U074TRF!E!SQYTRE!7M07L7UBTI4PR!FQS!RB
0IQB074LPRT47E7F24U07ILPQT20I7LBBFT7B7
QST07427BPLT24U0714BMBTI4PR!FQS!R7B7Q
S!7BT2!77777BBF!7B7QS!07427I7LBBF!7B7Q
S!07427 RT47E7F24U07IL7B7BIL4PBMF40B77
```

**7.** How many S's appear in the box?
- (A) 6
- (B) 8
- (C) 10
- (D) 12

**9.** How many M's appear in the box?
- (A) 4
- (B) 5
- (C) 6
- (D) 7

**8.** How many zeros (0) appear in the box?
- (A) 20
- (B) 23
- (C) 25
- (D) 33

## Box Four

```
4LPZT4/E/F24U0/ILPQT20I/L??FT/?/QST0/42/
?PLT24U0/I4?M?TI4PZ!FQS!Z/?/QS!/?T2!/////
??F!/?/QS!0/42/I/L??F!/?/QS!0/42/ ZT4/E/F24
U0/IL/?/?IL4P?MF40?//I4?M?TI4PZ!FQS!Z/?/Q
S!0/42Q0IL4P?M04F4YTZE!/M0/L/U?42YF2TE!
/F?M/IUWQ/S//20Q0Z?0IQ?0U4LPZT4/E/F24U
0/ILPQT20I/L04F4U0/4TZF!E!SQYTZE!/M0/L/U
?TI4PZ!FQS!Z?TZF!E!SQYTZE!/0IQ?0S
```

**10.** How many L's appear in the box?
- (A) 12
- (B) 13
- (C) 14
- (D) 15

**12.** How many S's appear in the box?
- (A) 12
- (B) 13
- (C) 14
- (D) 15

**11.** How many Z's appear in the box?
- (A) 12
- (B) 13
- (C) 14
- (D) 15

**BOX FIVE**

```
#LPZT#/E*F2#U0/ILPQT20I/L??FT&?/Q+T0/#2
*?PLT2#U0*I#?M?TI#PZ!FQ+!Z/?*Q+!&?T2!***
*&??F!*?*Q+!0*#2&I*L??F!&?/Q+!0/#2*ZT#*E
*F2#U0*IL&?*?IL#P?MF#0?**I#?M?TI#PZ!FQ+!
Z*?*Q+!0*#2Q0IL#P?M0#F#YTZE!&M0*L/U?#2
YF2TE!&F?M&IUWQ&+&/20Q0Z?0IQ?0U#LPZT#
*E/F2#U0*ILPQT20I/L0#F#U0/#TZF!E!+QYTZE
!/M0/L/U?TI#PZ!FQ+!Z?TZF!E!+QYT
```

**13.** How many plus signs (+) appear in the box?
- **(A)** 9
- **(B)** 11
- **(C)** 13
- **(D)** 15

**14.** How many slashes (/) appear in the box above?
- **(A)** 6
- **(B)** 8
- **(C)** 12
- **(D)** 16

**15.** How many F's appear in the box above?
- **(A)** 8
- **(B)** 16
- **(C)** 24
- **(D)** 30

# ANSWER KEY

## READING COMPREHENSION

1. **(A) is correct.** The passage is written with an impersonal objective tone, much like an article or news report, rather than to persuade or debate. It is not argumentative, passionate, or empathetic.

2. **(A) is correct.** In this context, *imperative* means "absolutely necessary." The passage asserts that "many people do not wish to move beyond this basic, instinctual level" of thought to critical thinking unless they must. It must be essential for them to engage in critical thinking, not just important or interesting (choices B and C). Choice D, *avoidable*, is not relevant here.

3. **(D) is correct.** Only I and III are true. Option II, which states critical thinking is *only* important in academia, contradicts the first sentence of paragraph 3: "Since the 1970s, critical thinking has also been used in police work." In fact, the point of the passage is that critical thinking is vital to police work (choice III).

4. **(B) is correct.** The definition of *savvy* is shrewd. This paragraph states that policing requires critical thinking to outsmart criminals. Choice A, *cool*, is not relevant here. *Inexperienced* is the opposite meaning; a savvy criminal would likely be quite experienced. And *dangerous* criminals are not necessarily savvy.

5. **(D) is correct.** If fewer crimes were successfully investigated and prosecuted since police began using critical thinking in investigations, then it would appear critical thinking is not helpful in police work. The purpose of paragraph 3 is to illustrate the many ways critical thinking has been used and can help in law enforcement. Answers A, B, and C are incorrect because they misstate facts or ideas from the passage.

6. **(B) is correct.** The best title for this passage is "Critical Thinking and Law Enforcement." Although the passage defines critical thinking and illustrates its various applications, the bulk of the passage talks about the application of critical thinking to law enforcement. Thus answer B is the best choice.

7. **(D) is correct.** Each point was presented as an important reason critical thinking is used in law enforcement.

8. **(D) is correct.** The chief's letter identifies personal reasons why many people

cannot schedule exercise into their daily routines. It also mentions the "warriors" who do work out in the morning, and the liability issues around allowing staff to exercise during shifts. Thus, D is the best answer; the chief will help, but he puts the responsibility on the employee to manage his or her time.

9. **(A) is correct.** The tone of the letter is cordial. The letter uses mostly friendly and supportive words in a professional format. The chief begins his letter by applauding employees for wanting to meet standards. He clearly explains the reasoning for his own choices in changing policy by taking away food options and prohibiting exercise on meal breaks. While it is debatable whether those choices are good policy for the officers, the tone of the letter is not angry or overbearing, ruling out choices B and D. He does express enthusiasm for the "warriors" he already works out with and says they would "love" other officers to join them, but this is more enthusiastic than overbearing, ruling out choice C.

10. **(B) is correct.** As used in the passage, the chief implies the "warriors" who work out every morning with him show motivation, energy, and a willingness to do what it takes to fit exercise into their schedules. Warfare and weapons are irrelevant to this passage. Finally, the chief does not suggest that those who work out with him are exceptionally experienced; otherwise, he would not invite those officers looking to improve their fitness to join them.

11. **(D) is correct.** The chief notes both logistics and liability as reasons why he denied the request.

12. **(C) is correct.** The introduction to the passage states that most officers spend fifteen hours a day working and commuting. There are twenty-four hours in a day; fifteen subtracted from twenty-four leaves nine hours remaining.

13. **(A) is correct.** The author's main point is that bullying has increased in scope from years past. If the number of children being bullied has increased, this strengthens the author's argument. The author asserts that bullying occurs beyond school, thanks to technology, making answer choice B incorrect. The passage discusses SROs at length, so if there were less funding for SROs, the argument would be weakened, making C incorrect. Finally, the passage states that youth suicides are increasing, so choice D directly contradicts the passage, making it incorrect.

14. **(B) is correct.** According to the passage, "SROs talk to kids at particular schools regularly," so "officers are in a unique position to identify emerging issues and prevent them before they develop into greater problems." The passage never states that SROs arrest bullies, just that SROs "are stationed at the school and spend their time dealing with law enforcement issues." SROs do not offer training; they "receive training in issues that are unique to youth." The passage never states specifically that SROs show teachers how to identify bullies, just that all personnel work together "to ensure schools remain a safe place for kids to learn."

15. **(C) is correct.** The passage immediately asserts that technological advancement has made bullying more prevalent. The first paragraph states that "[b]ullying among children and adolescents has evolved…to cyberstalking children across city and state lines with the use of common electronic devices." The passage explains that school resource officers enhance safety at school, so B is not correct. Finally, the passage never mentions more negative behavior among

children or boredom as factors in bullying, ruling out answer choices A and D.

16. **(C) is correct.** The passage mentions that the varying size and scope of different agencies make it difficult for them to communicate with one another. If each agency used its own dedicated communication system, then these communication systems would be the reason for interagency communication problems rather than the variation in size and scope of the agencies. Choices A, B, and D support the author's argument, because they assert that the ability of an agency to communicate effectively is based on its size.

17. **(B) is correct.** The author does not make a judgment about any specific type of security agency. Therefore, it can be inferred from the passage that the author believes that size and scope of a security department or operation do not matter as long as the operation functions properly.

18. **(C) is correct.** *Monolithically* means *massively*. It can also mean *stonelike*, but in this context choice C is the better answer; the passage suggests the agency is massive in contrast to "small-scale." This comparison makes choice C better than choice B, *impenetrable*. *Minuscule*, choice D, means the opposite.

19. **(D) is correct.** The passage mentions security companies, law enforcement, and contractors as agencies employed as campus security.

20. **(A) is correct.** According to the passage, "because the nature and scope of each campus security department varies so widely, the level of communication with other security and law enforcement departments also varies, causing misunderstandings and errors in interdepartmental communication." The passage mentions the type and size of various security agencies as a reason communication is a problem, but the overarching problem is communication, so choice A is a better answer than choice B. The passage states that "educating the college community about campus life and being safe while in a home away from home" is the job of campus security, not a problem, making choice C incorrect. Finally, the author suggests "to begin creating universal standards" for protection. Universal standards are not a problem but are a possible solution to problems.

21. **(A) is correct.** The passage implies that officers must diligently investigate due to witness unreliability. The author states in paragraph 1 that officers "must rely on … statements from witnesses and involved parties … to draw conclusions about what actually occurred" during a crime, making choice B incorrect. Choice C is incorrect because that passage states in paragraph 2 that "[t]he most frequent type of unreliable information is mistaken perception," not individual bias. Finally, in paragraph 5, the author states, "It is the officer's duty to use critical thinking, deduction, and logical reasoning to determine what is or is not reliable and why," so choice D cannot be correct; some witnesses can be determined to be reliable.

22. **(B) is correct.** In paragraph 3, the author writes, "[w]hile some people have biases they are aware of, sometimes people have biases they are unaware of for a number of reasons." People are generally unaware of the bias they hold. The other answer choices are untrue.

23. **(D) is correct.** Dishonesty, mistaken perception, and bias are all mentioned in the passage as problems with witness reliability.

24. **(B) is correct.** The author's main point is that witnesses can be unreliable. In paragraph 1, the author states that "the information officers receive is often inaccurate either because the individual was mistaken in his or her perception, was biased, or was purposefully deceptive." The other answer choices are *reasons* witnesses can be unreliable.

25. **(C) is correct.** Paragraph 2 describes auditory occlusion as "a temporary loss or lessening of hearing; sounds are muted or unheard." While auditory occlusion is a sort of sensory disturbance, choice C is better than choice D because it offers a more precise definition. Choice A is incorrect because auditory occlusion is not a *total* loss of hearing, just a temporary loss or lessening of hearing. It is not associated with vision, making choice B incorrect.

26. **(C) is correct.** *Anomaly* means *abnormality*. In the passage, a *time anomaly* is an abnormality in experiencing time. A *commonality* is a shared trait, implying the opposite of *anomaly* in this context, making choice A incorrect. Choices B and D, *ambivalence* and *uncertainty*, have similar meanings and do not make sense here.

27. **(B) is correct.** *Blatant* means *flagrant*. Answer choice A, *obvious*, is close in meaning but is not the *best* answer, because it lacks the negative connotation of *flagrant*. Answers C and D, *subtle* and *implied*, are oppositional in meaning to *flagrant*.

28. **(B) is correct.** The overall point of the passage is that ranchers still suffer from cattle rustling. The passage addresses the issues of cost, meat certifications, and branding, but these are not the main ideas of the passage.

29. **(C) is correct.** The rancher lost $100,000. Multiply 100 cows by $1,000 per cow: 100 × 1000 = $100,000.

30. **(B) is correct.** According to paragraph 3, "CHP grades livestock on a step level from 1 to 5, with 1 being the lowest and 5 being the highest. The higher the meat's rating, the more natural, healthy, and flavorful it is, allowing the farmer to command a premium price."

31. **(C) is correct.** The passage says that a higher rating from the CHP results in a higher price for meat; the CHP recommends against branding, making C the best choice. In paragraph 4 it is stated that CHP claims "that branding animals is not humane." It can be inferred from this statement that branding hurts the animals, making choice A incorrect. In paragraph 3, the author writes, "[a]s farmers desire to return to natural and humane ways of farming and cattle raising, while also increasing their earnings potential, fewer farmers are branding their cattle." Clearly, branding *is* a major issue for ranchers, and it is unlikely that most ranchers brand their cattle in this climate, making B and D incorrect.

32. **(D) is correct.** Paragraph 1 mentions the points made in choices A, B, and C. The passage never discusses services to help addicts overcome addiction.

33. **(B) is correct.** *Diligently* means *persistently*. Choices A and C, *neglectful* and *unconcerned*, do not make sense; ranchers and law enforcement are clearly attentive and concerned about this issue. Choice D, *carefully*, has a slightly different meaning.

34. **(A) is correct.** In paragraph 2, the passage states that "[t]he problem for ranchers … is that it's fairly easy to avoid detection while selling stolen livestock at auction. Why? The cows often are not branded." However, paragraph 3 discusses how

higher ratings from the Certified Humane Project (CHP) mean meat fetches higher prices at market, and in paragraph 4 the author writes, "ranchers have a decision to make—protect the herd with brands or resist branding to achieve higher CHP step ratings." The passage never mentions addicts being members of the community, making choice B incorrect. It explicitly states that branding reduces the value of meat because it results in a lower rating from the CHP, making choice C incorrect. Finally, the CHP is presented as a partner, not an adversary, making choice D incorrect.

35. **(D) is correct.** The main point of the passage is to stimulate thought. It presents a difficult issue: prisoner release. It also addresses two perspectives, noting that "[s]ome people believe a person who has committed a crime is lost and can never be redeemed," while "[o]thers believe there are justifiable reasons why any given crime was committed, and thus very few people should go to jail or prison for extended times." The passage also asks the reader to consider how to support prisoners in the community. Answer B is incorrect because the passage does more than simply provide information—it poses questions in paragraph 2. Answers A and C are incorrect because the passage is objective in its presentation of information and opinion. It never chooses a perspective.

36. **(B) is correct.** Choice B best addresses the ideas of the passage, which discusses the details of reentry programs. The passage discusses multiple perspectives, making choice A incorrect. Answer C is incorrect because the passage does not mention how to decrease recidivism. Answer D is not the best choice because it is too vague.

37. **(C) is correct.** Answer C is the best choice since the passage discusses the value of collaboration among community stakeholders. Answers A and B are differing opinions explicitly stated in the passage. Answer D is an oversimplification; paragraph 4 states that "[r]e-entry programs have shown success in many communities" but that "the perceived level of success may be well above or well below expectations."

38. **(D) is correct.** Natural inclination. Answers A, B, and C are incorrect because each can be a natural inclination.

39. **(A) is correct.** Paragraph 2 provokes the reader into thinking more deeply about prisoner re-entry by asking direct questions, illustrating the depth of the issue. The author does not provide an example or supporting details, making choices B and D incorrect. The point of paragraph 2 is not avoidance but provocation, making choice C incorrect.

40. **(C) is correct.** To *redeem* means to "buy back," "recover," "exchange," or "reform." In this context, *redeemed* means "reformed."

# WRITING

## Grammar, Usage, and Structure

1. **(B) is correct.** *Has* is a singular verb, referring to a singular noun (Neptune); *seasons* is the direct object of the verb *has*. *Seasons* must be plural to take the plural verb *last*.

2. **(C) is correct.** The plural verb *are* agrees with its plural subject *paintings*. The sentence has no error.

3. **(B) is correct.** A comma should never separate a subject (Nile River) from its verb (passes) without an interceding appositive.

4. **(D) is correct.** *Presidential* is an adjective that modifies the common noun *election*; neither word should be capitalized.

5. **(D) is correct.** *Mountain's* is not possessive in this sentence. It functions as a plural noun (mountains) so it does not require an apostrophe.

6. **(B) is correct.** Because the sentence states a general fact (how seat belts work), it should be written in present (or past) tense. The verb must be plural, since its subject, *Engineers*, is plural.

7. **(D) is correct.** The sentence already contains a negative ("The employer decided he could not...") so the modifier must be *any*; using a phrase like "no other benefits" would create an incorrect double negative.

8. **(D) is correct.** Choice D is the only correctly punctuated sentence. A comma correctly sets off the introductory phrase, and a period correctly ends the sentence. No colons or apostrophes are needed in this sentence; *its* should be possessive, meaning it should have no apostrophe.

9. **(B) is correct.** *And also functioned* introduces the second part of a compound verb phrase (*was created and functioned*).

10. **(A) is correct.** The comma is not needed to separate *such as* from the list it introduces.

11. **(A) is correct.** *Its* is a singular possessive pronoun, used here to refer to the *beaches* of the singular subject *Puerto Rico*.

12. **(A) is correct.** *Animals* is plural, so it does not agree with the singular pronoun *it*.

13. **(A) is correct.** *Grandchildren* and *cousins* are plural and so take the plural pronoun *their*.

14. **(D) is correct.** The second *parents* is plural, not possessive, so it does not require an apostrophe.

15. **(C) is correct.** *Are* is a present-tense plural helping verb describing the actions of the plural subject *countries*.

16. **(A) is correct.** *President* is a title and should be capitalized when it refers to a specific person.

17. **(B) is correct.** *Their* is a plural possessive referring to the antecedent *storm chasers*, which is also plural.

18. **(B) is correct.** The verb *is* agrees with the closest subject—in this case, the singular noun *brother*.

19. **(D) is correct.** Because of the language used later in the sentence ("still being released every year"), a present-tense verb is needed here ("*continues* to haunt"). It must be singular to match *assassination*.

20. **(A) is correct.** *Whose* is a possessive pronoun referring to the members.

## Clarity

1. **(B) is correct.** Answer A is a run-on sentence.

2. **(A) is correct.** Answer B contains a vague reference. It is not clear whose supervisor wishes to speak with which employee.

3. **(A) is correct.** Answer B contains a sentence fragment: "As she made the right turn."

4. **(B) is correct.** Answer A contains a misplaced modifier. It is not clear if officers who train are caught off guard infrequently, or if officers who train infrequently are caught off guard. Answer B is a clearer sentence.

5. **(A) is correct.** Answer B is a run-on sentence.

6. **(A) is correct.** Answer B contains a sentence fragment; the phrase "Than those who do not unless they are assigned to special covert details that have little contact with ordinary citizens" is not a complete sentence.

7. **(B) is correct.** Answer A contains a sentence fragment ("In the leg").

8. **(A) is correct.** Answer B is a run-on sentence. It requires a semicolon after *common goals*, or the sentence should be broken up into two as in answer choice A.

9. **(B) is correct.** Answer A contains a misplaced modifier and is unclear. Choice A states, "Detective Sherman *almost* got convictions," which implies he got acquittals instead. Choice B is clearer, as the word *almost* modifies *every arrest*, rather than *convictions*.

10. **(A) is correct.** Answer B contains a sentence fragment: "When dealing with family issues."

11. **(B) is correct.** Answer choice A contains a vague reference; it is not clear whether singing, dancing, acting, or all three made Kyle happy. Choice B is clearer.

12. **(A) is correct.** Answer B is a run-on sentence. The sentence should be broken up into two, as in answer choice A, or connected with a semicolon after *America*.

13. **(B) is correct.** Answer choice A contains a dangling modifier. The phrase "While happily at work downtown" is modifying "Marta's house" instead of Marta. It appears as if "Marta's house" is "happily at work."

14. **(A) is correct.** Answer choice B contains a misplaced modifier. It is not clear whether the officers or the fingerprints are on the print cards. Choice A is written more clearly, with *Officers* as the subject and using the active verb *collected*.

15. **(A) is correct.** Answer choice B contains a vague reference, using the pronoun *it*. It is not clear what Fran kept hidden. Answer choice A is more clearly written, specifying what Fran kept hidden: "her fear."

16. **(B) is correct.** Sentence A contains a sentence fragment ("Too fast").

17. **(B) is correct.** Sentence A contains a misplaced modifier: "on the way to work." It appears as though Steven's car, not Steven, is "on the way to work."

18. **(A) is correct.** Sentence B is a run-on sentence requiring punctuation after "party."

19. **(B) is correct.** Sentence A contains a vague reference. Officer Daryn says he does not like to drive fast but references an unspecified "you" in the sentence.

Sentence B clearly states that it is Officer Daryn who gets sick at high speeds.

20. **(B) is correct.** Sentence A contains a sentence fragment. "Unless they become a party to an action" is a dependent clause and must be connected to the preceding sentence with punctuation.

21. **(A) is correct.** Sentence B contains a vague reference: "he." It is unclear whether the judge or the defendant was remanded into custody.

22. **(B) is correct.** Sentence A is a run-on sentence. A semicolon is required after "staff," or a period should be inserted and a new sentence begun, as in sentence B.

23. **(B) is correct.** Sentence A contains a vague reference. Jack calls the Sheriff's Office, which is a business comprised of more than one person but is itself a singular unit; therefore, the use of the pronoun "they" is improper. Sentence B is clearer.

24. **(B) is correct.** Sentence A contains a sentence fragment. The phrase "That barks all hours of the day and night" is dependent on the sentence "Greg's neighbor has a dog."

25. **(A) is correct.** Sentence B contains a misplaced modifier, the phrase "by Officer Martinez." It appears that Officer Martinez stole the car. Sentence A is written more clearly to show that Officer Martinez made the report.

26. **(B) is correct.** Sentence A is a run-on sentence requiring punctuation after "concept."

27. **(B) is correct.** Sentence A contains a misplaced modifier. The phrase "eagerly awaiting time off" is a dangling modifier modifying "Ebony's vacation" rather than "Ebony," making it appear that the vacation, not the person, was waiting for time off.

28. **(B) is correct.** Sentence A is a run-on sentence. Punctuation is required after "safety."

29. **(A) is correct.** Sentence B contains a misplaced modifier: "in bags." It is unclear whether the lunches or the deputies were in bags.

30. **(B) is correct.** Sentence A contains a vague reference. It is unclear to whom "they" refers. This sentence illustrates an improper use of the pronoun "they."

## Vocabulary

### Synonyms

1. **(C) is correct.** *Apathetic* means *indifferent*. Omari might also be unsatisfied with his work, but *dissatisfied* is not the best answer here. He is the opposite of *motivated*. If he were *unsure* about his work, he might not be so quick to leave it.

2. **(B) is correct.** *Callous* means *insensitive*. A person may be *mean* or *annoyed* without being insensitive, so answer choices A and C are not the best choices. Answer choice D—*empathetic*—means the opposite of *callous* or *insensitive*.

3. **(D) is correct.** To *hinder* means to *impede*. To *impede* is less severe than to *crush*, which is to destroy something. Both *encourage* and *expedite* imply helping something to happen, which is the opposite meaning.

4. **(A) is correct.** *Pilfering* means *stealing*. If John had been *borrowing*, *moving*, or *returning* the newspaper, it is unlikely that Larry would have taken such drastic action.

5. **(C) is correct.** *Inconspicuous* means *unnoticeable*. Answer choice B, *prominent*, means the opposite. Answer choices A and D—*large* and *small*—are not the best choices because both large and small items *could* be inconspicuous.

6. **(A) is correct.** *Belligerent* means *hostile*. The other answer choices—*sad*, *angry*, and *loud*—are not the best answers because a person may exhibit any of those characteristics without being hostile or combative.

7. **(B) is correct.** *Lucid* means *rational* or *clear*. Answer choices A and D—*confused* and *incomprehensible*—are the opposite of *rational*. Clyde may have been *emotional*, but that does not explain why he was able to describe a person while in a stressful situation.

8. **(A) is correct.** *Frantic* means *frenzied*. Choice B, *calm*, is the opposite of *frantic*; it is unlikely a father would be calm if he realized his child was missing. Answers C and D—*frustrated* and *upset*—are both incorrect because it is possible to be frustrated or upset without being frantic.

9. **(C) is correct.** *Exacerbated* means *aggravated*, to make something worse. Answer choice A, *hurt*, is not relevant here; it is not possible to "hurt" a problem. Answer B, *reduced*, means the opposite of *exacerbated*. Choice D, *excited*, lacks the negative connotation of *exacerbated*.

10. **(D) is correct.** *Verbose* means *wordy*. *Concise* is the opposite of *wordy*. Choices B and C, *clear* and *confusing*, are not the best choices because a text can be clear or confusing while being verbose at the same time.

11. **(D) is correct.** To *foster* means to *promote*. Choice B, *create*, is incorrect because it implies the relationships do not yet exist. Choices A and C, *alleviate* and *discourage*, imply the opposite of *promote*.

12. **(A) is correct.** To *quantify* is to *measure* or count the value of something. Quantifying something might make it more *understandable*, but answer choice A, *measure*, is the best answer here.

13. **(B) is correct.** *Dubious* means *questionable*. *Dishonest*, answer choice A, is not the same as *dubious*; something can be questionable while still being the truth. Answer choice C, *obvious*, is unrelated in meaning. Answer choice D, *definite*, implies certainty, the opposite of *dubious*.

14. **(A) is correct.** *Furtively* means *stealthily*. *Fraudulently*, choice B, is unrelated. Answers C and D, *brazenly* and *openly*, are antonyms of *furtively*.

15. **(B) is correct.** To *hone* is to *sharpen*. *Build* and *improve* are close in meaning to *hone* but are not synonyms. *Steady* is unrelated.

## Antonyms

1. **(B) is correct.** *Intermittent* is the opposite of *persistent*. Answers A and C, *lasting* and *unrelenting*, are synonyms. *Harsh* is unconnected because both an intermittent and a persistent cough could be harsh.

2. **(C) is correct.** *Submits* is the opposite of *supersede*. *Overrides* is a synonym for *supersedes*. *Supports* and *boosts* are closer in meaning to *supersedes*, though not exactly the same, as they fail to imply the sense of overruling; in any case, they are not opposite in meaning to *supersedes*.

3. **(B) is correct.** *Bolster* is the opposite of *mitigate*. Answer A, *lessen*, is a synonym.

The other choices, *extend* and *change*, do not relate to *mitigate*.

4. **(B) is correct.** *Abdicated* is an antonym of *maintained*. Answer choice D, *relinquished*, is a synonym. Choice A, *left*, lacks the implication of a responsible departure; when relinquishing a position, the office holder gives it up to another. Likewise, answer choice C, *abandoned*, is close in meaning but overly extreme; someone can *relinquish* a position or role without leaving irresponsibly.

5. **(D) is correct.** *Deviate* is the opposite of *remain*. The other answer choices—*diverge*, *depart*, and *sway*—are synonyms of *diverge*.

6. **(C) is correct.** *Guile* is the opposite of *honesty*. Answer A, *duplicity*, is a synonym. *Assistance*, choice B, is unrelated in meaning and does not make sense in context. Answer D, *savvy*, means "clever"; someone can be savvy but still be honest.

7. **(C) is correct.** *Repealed* means *revoked* (choice A, a synonym). *Added* would imply the opposite. *Understood* and *arranged* do not make sense in this context.

8. **(A) is correct.** To *disavow* is "to deny"; its antonym is *admit*. *Dismissed* and *refused* are essentially synonyms for *disavowed* here; *wondered* does not make sense.

## Fill in the Blank

1. **(B) is correct.** In this context, *course* means "manner of procedure." *Coarse* is a homonym and means "harsh" or "grating."

2. **(B) is correct.** In this context, *serial* means "producing a series of similar actions," such as killing. *Cereal* is an edible grain.

3. **(A) is correct.** *Effect* as used in this context is a noun. Generally (though there are exceptions), the word *affect* is a verb, and *effect* is a noun. To *affect* is to "act upon something to cause change," as in "The snow *affected* his ability to drive." An *effect* is a result, as in "The snow had a negative *effect* on the undercarriage of his car." In the exam question, the "increased penalties" had no *effect* on crime.

4. **(A) is correct.** *Incite* means to "urge" or "encourage." *Insight* is "the ability to see an underlying truth."

5. **(A) is correct.** To *know* means to "have knowledge" of something. *No* is used to show dissent or denial.

6. **(B) is correct.** *Steal* means to "take another's property without permission." *Steel* is a type of metal.

7. **(A) is correct.** *Principles*, "codes, morals, doctrines," are nouns. *Principal* is a noun when it refers to a person, like the head of a school; otherwise it is an adjective.

## Spelling

### Choose the Correct Spelling

1. **(C) is correct** (toward).

2. **(D) is correct** (liaison).

3. **(C) is correct** (rescinded).

4. **(A) is correct** (surprised).

5. **B) is correct.** (tendency).

6. **(A) is correct.** (necessary).

7. **(D) is correct.** (government).

8. **(B) is correct** (palpable).

9. **(A) is correct** (interrogated).

10. **(B is correct** (independent).

11. **(C) is correct** (subpoena).

12. **(D) is correct** (suspicious).

13. **(C) is correct** (facilitate).

14. **(A) is correct** (heinous).

15. **(D) is correct** (incorrigible).

16. **(A) is correct** (tenacious).

17. **(B) is correct** (perfunctory).

18. **(A) is correct** (seditious).

19. **(B) is correct** (surveillance).

20. **(D) is correct** (vagrancy).

### Identifying Spelling Errors

1. **(D) is correct.** Choice D, *harrassing*, is spelled incorrectly. It should be spelled *harassing*.

2. **(C) is correct.** Choice C, *accommadations*, is spelled incorrectly. It should be spelled *accommodations*.

3. **(B) is correct.** Choice B, *noticably*, is spelled incorrectly. It should be spelled *noticeably*.

4. **(C) is correct.** Choice C, *possesion*, is spelled incorrectly. It should be spelled *possession*.

5. **(A) is correct.** Choice A, *seige*, is spelled incorrectly. It should be spelled *siege*.

6. **(B) is correct.** Choice B, *publically*, is spelled incorrectly. It should be spelled *publicly*.

7. **(D) is correct.** Choice D, *agressive*, is spelled incorrectly. It should be spelled *aggressive*.

8. **(D) is correct.** Choice D, *flourescent*, is spelled incorrectly. It should be spelled *fluorescent*.

9. **(C) is correct.** Choice C, *advirsareal*, is spelled incorrectly. It should be spelled *adversarial*.

10. **(B) is correct.** Choice B, *germain*, is spelled incorrectly. It should be spelled *germane*.

### Cloze

#### Cloze One

More than twenty-five years ago, law enforcement first partnered with community leaders in an attempt to bridge the gap between the police and the communities they serve. Law enforcement had long since realized **S O C I E T A L** changes were making it more and **M O R E** difficult to do the job without **C O M M U N I T Y** support. Because police could not do **T H E** job alone, and thus did the **J O B** poorly in certain communities, community trust **B E G A N** to falter. The creation of community **P O L I C I N G** programs was a way to rebuild **T H E** community trust as well as to reinvigorate **I T** and allow police to do their **J O B** better. Initial community policing programs were **P R I M A R I L Y** designed to help community members mobilize **S U P P O R T** and resources to solve problems, voice **T H E I R** concerns, contribute advice, and take action **T O** address concerns. But these initial programs tended to be paternalistic, and while some **C O M M U N I T I E S** showed improvement, the improvement was slow. **I N** other communities, residents and leaders outright **R E S I S T E D** the efforts of the police to **W O R K** together.

Over the years, community policing **EVOLVED**. This evolution reflected moving away from the paternalism of **OLD** programs and toward more true collaboration. **RATHER** than simply "voicing opinions," which police **THEN** took under advisement while determining an action **PLAN**, community members became bona fide stakeholders **WITH** equal control over community priorities and **ACTION** plans. Today, community policing exists as **A** collaborative effort between police and these community **STAKEHOLDERS** such as schools, community-based organizations, local large and small **BUSINESSES**, local government, and residents, and is designed to **IDENTIFY**, prioritize, and solve community problems. Across the United States, the **NATIONAL** community policing philosophy promotes organizational strategies **THAT** use this collaboration to problem-solve **AND** proactively address persistent or emerging public **SAFETY** problems such as crime and social **DISORDER**. All current community programs must be **BASED** on three essential components: **COLLABORATIVE** partnerships; organizational transformation to support these collaborative partnerships as well as to support **PROBLEM**-solving methods; and a proactive, systemic **EXAMINATION** of identified issues. This examination should also explore effective response evaluation. As a **RESULT**, models of community policing exist in most police agencies across the nation and the communities they serve, crisis situations have decreased in many communities, and the police have a markedly improved relationship with the citizens they **SERVE**.

## Cloze Two

All law enforcement officers are sworn in to the office using a standard oath. Each new officer proudly swears that **HE** or she will never betray his **OR** her badge, integrity, character, or the **PUBLIC** trust, and to uphold all laws **AND** the United States Constitution. Every officer **TAKES** this oath seriously. Most officers will never **FORGET** the day that badge was handed **TO** them and they raised their right **HAND**.

The oath is not the only **PROMISE** an officer makes every day he or she **PUTS** on the badge. At each agency there **ARE** daily reminders of core values, traditions, **CARDINAL** rules, the police officers' prayer, and **SO** on. The tenets of each are fairly the same and give an officer **A** sense of pride about the job. **ANOTHER** such promise is the police officer **CODE** of ethics. The officer code of **ETHICS** takes the promise a little further, **AWAY** from the law and toward a **MORE** humanitarian purpose. In the code of **ETHICS**, an officer affirms that his or her "fundamental duty" **IS** to serve humankind, to defend the **WEAK** and defenseless against oppression or intimidation, **AND** the peaceful against violence and disorder.

It is this last sentence that **IS** most striking. In the midst of **UNREST** around the nation, many might assume **THE** officers' role is to intimidate and **OPPRESS** rather than to prevent. Is **IT** possible then for chaos, violence, and **DISORDER** to coexist with peacefulness in the **SAME** space, such that any attempt to address violence will not necessarily and negatively **AFFECT** the peaceful?

And, if so, how **IS** it possible for an officer to **ADHERE** to the oath and the code? **HOWEVER**, maybe there are two sides to **THE** proverbial coin, and both sides of **THE** truth are true, even if they may seem to conflict. Meanwhile, **ONE** can only hope for guidance. We hope also that as we attempt to navigate issues of violence, peace, civil disobedience, and **SOCIAL** disorder amid the anger, frustration, and mistrust for one another, officers will continue to remember the overwhelming pride and honor felt the day that badge was handed to them, they raised their **RIGHT** hand, and **SWORE** always to do the right thing.

# MATHEMATICS

## Mathematical Operations

1. **(A) is correct.** Multiply 6 by 20 (6 × 20 = 120), 3 by 10 (3 × 10 = 30), and 4 by 1 (4 × 1 = 4) to get 120 + 30 + 4 = **154**.

2. **(D) is correct.** Multiply 20 by 100 to get 2000: 20 × 100 = **2000**.

3. **(C) is correct.** Divide 240 by 8 to get 30: 240 ÷ 8 = **30**.

4. **(B) is correct.** Multiply the number of hours worked (4) by 22: 4 × 22 = 88. Then, add 50 to 88: 50 + 88 = **$138**.

5. **(B) is correct.** Each demerit represents a loss of 7 points, or –7. If an officer lost 7 points 3 times, that means the officer would have lost a total of 21 points, or **–21**.

6. **(A) is correct.** (–15) – 8 = **–23°F**

7. **(C) is correct.** 235 – 178 = 57, so the fine is **$57** more.

## Fractions, Decimals, and Percentages

1. **(A) is correct.** Twenty divided by 7 gives the improper fraction of $2\frac{6}{7}$.
$\frac{20}{7} = \mathbf{2\frac{6}{7}}$

2. **(B) is correct.** Multiply 340 by 0.15: 340 × 0.15 = **$51**

3. **(B) is correct.** Subtract $1\frac{7}{8}$ from $2\frac{3}{4}$:
$2\frac{3}{4} - 1\frac{7}{8} = 2\frac{6}{8} - 1\frac{7}{8} = 1\frac{14}{8} - 1\frac{7}{8} = \mathbf{\frac{7}{8}}$

4. **(D) is correct.** 230.5 – 187.9 = 42.6, or **$42.60**.

5. **(D) is correct.** Multiply $2\frac{1}{2}$ by $\frac{1}{4}$:
$2\frac{1}{2} \times \frac{1}{4} = \frac{5}{2} \times \frac{1}{4} = \mathbf{\frac{5}{8}}$

6. **(C) is correct.** Divide 150 by one-third:
$\frac{150}{1} \div \frac{1}{3} = \frac{150}{1} \times \frac{3}{1} = \mathbf{450}$

7. **(A) is correct.** 4.5 + 1.45 + 2.45 = 8.4, or **$8.40**.

## Ratios and Proportions

1. **(A) is correct.** There are 40 men to 30 women. This simplifies to 4:3.
70 – 40 = 30 woman police officers
$\frac{40}{30} = \frac{4}{3}$ or **4:3**

2. **(A) is correct.** There were a total of 300 arrests. Subtracting the 50 arrests for disorderly conduct gives 250 arrests for other offenses (300 – 50 = 250). Therefore, you can write the ratio 50:250. If you divide both numbers by 50, you get the ratio of **1:5**.

3. **(C) is correct.** There are a total of 50 cadets. Subtracting the 20 cadets who do have children gives 30 cadets who do not have children (50 – 20 = 30 cadets who do not have children). The ratio can be written as 20:30. Since the common denominator is 10, the ratio can be reduced to **2:3**.

4. **(B) is correct.**

| | |
|---|---|
| $\frac{7 \text{ blocks}}{30 \text{ mins}} = \frac{10 \text{ blocks}}{x \text{ min}}$ | Solve the proportion. |
| $7x = 10(30)$ | Cross multiply. |

ANSWER KEY 133

| | |
|---|---|
| $7x = 300$ | Divide both sides by 7. |
| $x = 42.86 \approx 43$ | Round to approximately 43 minutes. |

5. **(C) is correct.**

| | |
|---|---|
| $\frac{5}{8} = \frac{x}{120}$ | Solve the proportion. |
| $8x = 5(120)$ | Cross multiply. |
| $8x = 600$ | Divide both sides by 8. |
| $x = 75$ | Solve. |

6. **(D) is correct.**

| | |
|---|---|
| $\frac{7}{17.5} = \frac{12}{x}$ | Solve the proportion. |
| $7x = 12(17.5)$ | Cross multiply. |
| $7x = 210$ | Divide both sides by 7. |
| $x = 30$ | Solve. |

## Estimation and Rounding

1. **(C) is correct.** $441.78 rounds to $440, and $178.12 rounds to $180: $440 + $180 = **$620**.

2. **(A) is correct.** $245.90 rounds up to $250: $4 \times \$250 = \textbf{\$1000}$.

3. **(A) is correct.** $45.89 rounds up to 46; $17.90 rounds up to 18; and $5.78 rounds up to 6: 46 + 18 + 6 = **$70**.

4. **(D) is correct.** $283.96 rounds to 280, and $38.12 rounds to 40: 280 + 40 = **$320**.

5. **(B) is correct.** $145,893.45 rounds up to $146,000. The 893 rounds up to 900, making 145,900; the 9 in the hundreds place causes the 5 in the thousands place to round up as well, making **$146,000**.

6. **(B) is correct.** The 7 in the tens place causes the 3 in the hundreds place to round up: 61,370 becomes **61,400**.

## Units

1. **(D) is correct.** Each mile has 1760 yards: 1760 yds × 2 = **3520 yds.**

2. **(C) is correct.** There are 16 ounces in a pound: 35 lbs. × 16 oz. = **560 oz.**

3. **(B) is correct.** There are 2000 pounds in a ton: 1.2 × 2000 lbs = **2400 lbs.**

4. **(C) is correct.** There are 1000 meters in a kilometer: 5 × 1000 = **5000 m**

5. **(D) is correct.** First, determine how many months the inmate will serve. There are 12 months in a year: 5.5 × 12 = 66 months. According to the question, there are 30 days in a month: 66 × 30 days = **1980 days**.

6. **(A) is correct.** There are 60 minutes in an hour. Use the formula $\frac{distance}{time}$ = rate: $\frac{2}{17}$ = 0.1176. Then multiply by 60: 60 × 0.1176 = 7.056. Round to the nearest number: 7.056 ≈ **7 mph**.

7. **(A) is correct.** There are 1000 grams in a kilogram: 1700 / 1000 = **1.7 kg**.

## Perimeter and Area

1. **(C) is correct.**

   | | |
   |---|---|
   | $A = l \times w$ | Use the formula for area of a rectangle. |
   | 40 yd × 70 yd | Multiply. |
   | = **2800 yd²** | Solve. |

2. **(B) is correct.**

   | | |
   |---|---|
   | $A = \frac{1}{2}bh$ | Use the formula for area of a triangle. |
   | 3 cm × 5 cm | Multiply. |
   | = 15 cm ÷ 2 | Divide by 2. |
   | = **7.5 cm²** | Solve. |

3. **(A) is correct.**

   | | |
   |---|---|
   | $C = 2\pi r$ | Use the formula for circumference. |
   | $r = \frac{170}{2} = 85$ | To find the radius, divide the diameter by 2. |
   | $C = 2\pi 85$ | Plug in the variables and solve. |
   | C = **533.8 yd** | Solve. |

4. **(A) is correct.** Since the block is a square, we are looking for a number that is multiplied by itself to give 40,000. In math, that is called the *square root*. The square root of 40,000 is 200: $\sqrt{40{,}000}$ = **200**. To check the answer, apply the formula for the area of a square ($A = s^2$): 200 × 200 = 40,000.

5. **(D) is correct.**

   | | |
   |---|---|
   | $P = s_1 + s_2 + s_3 + \ldots s_n$ | Use the formula for perimeter. |
   | 5.1 cm + 5.1 cm + 5.1 cm + 5.1 cm + 5.1 cm **OR** 5.1 cm × 5 | In this regular pentagon, each side measures the same length. A pentagon has 5 sides. |
   | = **25.5 cm** | Solve. |

6. **(B) is correct.**

   | | |
   |---|---|
   | $P = s_1 + s_2 + s_3 + \ldots s_n$ | Use the formula for perimeter. |
   | 100 yd + 100 yd + 30 yd + 30 yd | A football field is shaped like a rectangle (two long sides, two short sides). |
   | = **260 yd** | Solve. |

7. **(C) is correct.**

   | | |
   |---|---|
   | $A = l \times w$ | Use the formula for area of a rectangle. |
   | 10 ft × 12 ft | Multiply. |
   | = **120 ft²** | Solve. |

# REASONING

## Inductive Reasoning

1. **(A) is correct.** Both burglaries and robberies increase and peak at 12:00 a.m.

2. **(C) is correct.** The sharpest decline in robberies and burglaries occurs between 12:00 a.m. and 2:00 a.m. The decline between 2:00 a.m. and 4:00 a.m. is not as dramatic.

3. **(D) is correct.** While the number of burglaries plummets at 10:00 p.m., the number of robberies is still quite high, so the best answer is 6:00 a.m., when both crimes, on average, are at their lowest.

4. **(A) is correct.** While the decrease in crime continues through 9:00 p.m., the graph shows that this trend begins at 8:00 p.m.

5. **(D) is correct.** According to the graph, crime peaks around 12:00 a.m., which means that any time frame including 12:00 a.m. is incorrect. Crime is shown to decrease between 2:00 a.m. and 6:00 a.m.

6. **(A) is correct.** According to the graph, the state police carried out close to eighty stops between January and March before climbing close to one hundred stops in April and May.

7. **(C) is correct.** The graph shows that both the state police and municipal police had one hundred or more stops in April.

8. **(D) is correct.** According to the graph, the state and municipal police issued nearly the same number of stops in February (approximately eighty) and April (approximately one hundred).

9. **(D) is correct.** Stops reached a five-month high for state police in May, climbing to over one hundred.

10. **(A) is correct.** Municipal police stops were at their lowest (below forty) in January.

11. **(B) is correct.** The sharpest decrease occurs from July (the likely all-time high) to August.

12. **(C) is correct.** The DUIs decreased from a high of one hundred to between seventy and eighty incidents. The best answer is a twenty-four–incident decrease. In October, there were only about seventy-five or seventy-six DUI incidents; 100 − 76 = 24.

13. **(A) is correct.** There were one hundred DUI incidents in July, more than any other month.

14. **(D) is correct.** October is the only month with fewer than eighty DUIs.

15. **(C) is correct.** August and September have the closest data points, hovering close to eighty DUIs, while July and October are outliers.

## Deductive Reasoning

1. **(C) is correct.** The only rule followed was that the meeting took place in the chief's conference room. The meeting was not conducted at a reasonable hour; it was after an overnight shift. The officer's Statement of Rights was not read, the meeting and did not offer breaks, and the captain denied the officer the right to record the meeting.

2. **(B) is correct.** The board did not read a Statement of Rights.

3. **(A) is correct.** The board correctly followed all five steps of the State Code.

4. **(A) is correct.** According to the rules and regulations, "whenever an agency member is suspended without pay, they may appeal this disciplinary action within one (1) month of their suspension."

5. **(B) is correct.** According to the rules and regulations, during an investigation, an employee will be placed on leave, but with pay.

6. **(A) is correct.** According to the rules and regulations, "whenever an agency member is demoted, they may appeal this disciplinary action within one (1) month of their demotion."

7. **(B) is correct.** The range of disciplinary action for excessive loitering in the workplace is written warning to suspension.

8. **(B) is correct.** The required disciplinary action for threatening to overthrow the government or joining an anti-government group is automatic discharge.

9. **(B) is correct.** The range of disciplinary action for unauthorized use of a weapon is suspension to discharge.

10. **(D) is correct.** The required disciplinary action for three consecutive absences without administrative approval is compulsory resignation.

11. **(A) is correct.** The range of disciplinary action for insubordination is written warning to suspension. Since this is Officer Gordon's first offense, he will likely receive a reprimand.

12. **(B) is correct.** The last step Officer Morrison took was running the license plate to determine whether the car is stolen. Since the car is not stolen, the next step should be to contact the vehicle's owner(s).

13. **(D) is correct.** Officer McNamara forgot to contact the vehicle's owner(s).

14. **(D) is correct.** According to protocol, Officer White should carry out a field sobriety assessment to determine whether the individual is intoxicated.

15. **(A) is correct.** Officer Del Rio "reserves the right to confiscate a driver's license if they refuse to take a blood alcohol test."

## Problem Sensitivity

1. **(C) is correct.** Officer Brown's restless, anxious, shaking, and erratic behaviors—combined with the dilated and bloodshot eyes and the apparent presence of pills without a prescription—are all signs of possible drug use.

2. **(D) is correct.** Medication is usually provided in a prescription bottle or package. It is suspicious that Brown has a bag of pills that don't appear to have a prescription—especially since Brown tried to conceal the pills. It is possible that they are illicit.

3. **(B) is correct.** It is most likely that Officer Brown apologized to Officer Singh to repair their relationship after being caught concealing pills.

4. **(D) is correct.** Kelly Zicchardo "heard someone shout, 'Drop your weapon!' [and] remembers looking at the cash register, and it said 7:07 p.m."

5. **(A) is correct.** The suspect is "known to be a local addict with a history of violence" and he already asked John Albright for "a fix or some cash."

6. **(D) is correct.** Jim Lord is the only person, other than Harry Cartwright, to be in proximity of the crime.

7. **(D) is correct.** The civilian might be the suspect, so it is important that Officer Crawley denies his requests to help but also engages him to uncover more information.

8. **(C) is correct.** Both Jack Cho and Arnie Haynes saw a tall, young man running away from a fire scene.

9. **(D) is correct.** Officer Gordon did not report the make and model of the vehicle.

10. **(D) is correct.** The suspicious-looking person matches the description of the burglar, so it is best practice to stop the man to gain more insight.

11. **(B) is correct.** The best approach would be to report this type of behavior to the commanding officer or another supervisor.

12. **(C) is correct.** Witness 3's information does not match the details of the information provided by the other three witnesses.

13. **(C) is correct.** Violations of protocol need to be reported, even in moments of emotional escalation. It is best to discuss the situation with your partner to maintain a productive working environment.

14. **(C) is correct.** Hesitation could be fatal for the victim.

15. **(A) is correct.** It is important to maintain all directives and protocols coming from supervisors.

## Spatial Orientation

1. **(B) is correct.** Officer Rockwood will make two right-hand turns to get to the park from the circular drive.

2. **(B) is correct.** Officer Rockwood will have to patrol three parks north of the Otago River: Waitiki Park, Golden Park, and Taupo Park.

3. **(A) is correct.** Officer Rockwood will have to patrol one park south of the Otago River: Riverside Park.

4. **(D) is correct.** Officer Rockwood will have to move west from where he is parked to respond to the crash.

5. **(A) is correct.** In this scenario, Officer Rockwood will encounter three four-way intersections on his journey.

6. **(B) is correct.** The Fulbright Monument is located due east from Officer Rockwood's location on the road north of Golden Park.

7. **(A) is correct.** Officer Rockwood will travel on two roads to make it back to the police station as quickly as possible.

8. **(B) is correct.** Officer Rue must make a right on Mountain Road to respond to this incident from his current location.

9. **(C) is correct.** There are three campgrounds near Lake Manitoba.

10. **(B) is correct.** Officer Rue would have to travel southeast in a straight line from his current location in order to reach the Clapper Forest.

11. **(D) is correct.** Officer Rue will drive on Pine Road, Park Road, and W. Lake Road to make it to the parking lot on W. Lake Road.

12. **(C) is correct.** Officer Rue will head east on W. Lake Road and south on Park Road to report to this trailhead.

13. **(D) is correct.** From his current location, Officer Rue will travel southwest to reach the southernmost campground in the park.

14. **(D) is correct.** From his current location, Officer Rue will travel west to reach the easternmost campground in the park.

15. **(B) is correct.** Officer Rue's best choice is to head north on the trail closest to his parking lot in order to reach Dunbar Forest quickly.

**Information Ordering**

1. **(A) is correct.** The most logical sequence is that the victim got off their shift, went for a walk on the boardwalk, was approached by the vagrant asking for money, refused the vagrant's request, and was assaulted as a result.

2. **(B) is correct.** The first five events set up the assault and robbery: the victim rounds the corner, sees Daniel, and tries to not interact with him. Daniel responds by not letting her pass and grabbing her arm. This is the only logical order for these events because each step is consequential; each event is reliant upon the details of the previous event.

3. **(A) is correct.** The assault and robbery must occur AFTER the five preceding events. Listing these events in reverse order would be illogical. The victim must run to the backyard before she can be chased there. She must be tackled before she can be on the ground. She must cry before she can be heard crying. And the neighbor must hear her before chasing Daniel away.

4. **(A) is correct.** The person must be searched before they can be handcuffed. They must be handcuffed before they can be placed in the police cruiser. And they must be fully detained before it is safe enough to notify dispatch.

5. **(B) is correct.** The two men must enter the gas station before they can commit the crime at gunpoint at the cash register. The cash must be requested before it is handed over. The police entered just as it was handed over, so their attempt to deter an escape would come after their entrance. The two men escaped just after the police told them to stop.

6. **(C) is correct.** The couple must be arguing before they can get the attention of everyone in the bar. The woman's brother would have to hear the argument before he could monitor it and intervene. The brother would likely threaten to stab the man before actually stabbing him.

7. **(C) is correct.** The older man would likely have to park the car and enter the school before the suspect in the red hooded sweatshirt could turn the corner and take advantage of the situation. The suspect would have to approach the car before he used the tool to break the window. The window had to be broken before the older man could hear it. He would likely have to come outside before he could yell at the young man.

8. **(A) is correct.** Heart failure is more threatening than the other injuries. Deep wound bleeding is more life-threatening than shock but less life-threatening than a heart attack. A non-protruding broken bone is more dangerous than minor lacerations but not quite as urgent as shock, deep wound bleeding, and heart failure. Minor lacerations are typically not of high concern.

ANSWER KEY 139

9. **(A) is correct.** She would have to see the teenagers before asking them a question. The teenagers would have to be asked a question before it could be ignored. They would have to be in the alleyway before causing damage. The breaking glass and booming sound would likely occur before the smoke and flames. She would likely have to see the teens running off from the smoke and flames before calling 911.

10. **(C) is correct.** The witnesses would have to see the fire from afar before they could see it up close. Once they got close, they would likely see the protesters with sledgehammers. The sledgehammers would have to break the statues' foundations before the statues began to collapse. And the witnesses would see the statues begin to collapse before they finally fell.

11. **(C) is correct.** The passage states, "The police arrived just as the first statue tumbled to the ground. The protesters scattered." It is reasonable to infer that the police scared the protesters away; the statue was already collapsing and the fire was already raging.

12. **(C) is correct.** Betty would have to enter the store first (at 3:00 a.m.). She would first obtain the milk before paying for it at the cash register. She had to have noticed the man before seeing him pull a gun. She would likely drop to the ground in response to seeing the gun.

13. **(C) is correct.** She sees the men arguing before she sees Bruce get shoved. Bruce would have to be shoved first in order to fall and hit his head. The man exited the side door *after* the assault, so that would be after Bruce hit his head. And she does not call the police until *after* the man leaves.

14. **(A) is correct.** The officer would have to register the firearms before entering the facility. The officer would then have to acquire the proper safety gear at the front desk. The officer would have to reach the firing area and fire before reloading. Equipment would be returned after all firing has been completed.

15. **(D) is correct.** The masked criminals would have to enter the fast-food restaurant before requesting valuables. The valuables were stolen before the police officer entered. The individuals fled because of the police officer. And the victim would remain on scene to give a statement *after* this occurred.

## Memorization

1. **(B) is correct.** The suspect is wearing jeans and a hooded sweatshirt.

2. **(D) is correct.** The subject is leaning against a squad car as one police officer frisks him.

3. **(C) is correct.** The female police officer is holding onto handcuffs with her left hand.

4. **(D) is correct.** There is a person (wearing black) lying on the ground in the upper-left-hand corner of the photograph.

5. **(B) is correct.** The officer is placing a marker labeled with the number 2 near the crime scene.

6. **(B) is correct.** There is one person lying on the ground in the upper-left-hand corner of the photo and there is also one officer.

7. **(C) is correct.** The person in the photograph has a brush in their right hand.

8. **(B) is correct.** There are two markers visible in the dirt.

9. **(C) is correct.** The log, dirt, and plants most likely are part of a wooded area.

10. **(C) is correct.** The handcuffs on the suspect indicate that the officer on the left is most likely detaining the suspect.

11. **(C) is correct.** There is a traffic cone visible to the left of the suspect, through the officer's legs.

12. **(C) is correct.** The suspect's face cannot be seen because it is facing away from the camera. It is not turned to the left or right.

13. **(D) is correct.** The back of the officer's vest says "NYPD."

14. **(A) is correct.** The car's front-end is pointing to the left of the photo, indicating that it is most likely driving from right to left.

15. **(C) is correct.** The officer is standing at an intersection, close to a crosswalk, indicating that he is likely directing traffic. The officer also has a traffic vest and gloves on.

## Visualization

1. **(C) is correct.**
2. **(A) is correct.**

## Selective Attention

1. **(B) is correct.**
2. **(A) is correct.**
3. **(C) is correct.**
4. **(D) is correct.**
5. **(B) is correct.**
6. **(A) is correct.**
7. **(C) is correct.**
8. **(B) is correct.**
9. **(D) is correct.**
10. **(C) is correct.**
11. **(B) is correct.**
12. **(D) is correct.**
13. **(B) is correct.**
14. **(C) is correct.**
15. **(C) is correct.**

## Flexibility of Closure

1. **(D) is correct.** Twelve question marks (?) appear in the box.

```
I?BMBTIOPRDFQSDRABCQSDJAOGQJILOPBMJ?
F?YTREDCMJALAUB?GYFGTEDCFBMAIUWQASXC
GJQJILOPBMJ?F?UJA?TRFDEDSQYTREDCMJALA
UBTIOPRDFQSDRBJIQBJUOLPRTOAECFG?UJAIL
PQTGJIALBBFDABCQSDJAOGCBPLTG?UJAI?BMB
TIOPRDFQSDRABCQSDJAOGCBDRBJIQBJUOLPR
TOAECFG?UJAILPQTGJIALBBFDABCQSDJAOGC
IALBBFDABCQSDJAOGCRTOAECFG?UJAILABAB
```

2. **(B) is correct.** Twenty-nine A's appear in the box.

   I?BMBTIOPRDFQSDR**A**BCQSDJ**A**OGQJILOPBMJ?
   F?YTREDCMJ**A**L**A**UB?GYFGTEDCFBM**A**IUWQ**A**SXC
   GJQJILOPBMJ?F?UJ**A**?TRFDEDSQYTREDCMJ**A**L**A**
   UBTIOPRDFQSDRBJIQBJUOLPRTO**A**ECFG?UJ**A**IL
   PQTGJI**A**LBBFD**A**BCQSDJ**A**OGCBPLTG?UJ**A**I?BMB
   TIOPRDFQSDR**A**BCQSDJ**A**OGCBDRBJIQBJUOLPR
   TO**A**ECFG?UJ**A**ILPQTGJI**A**LBBFD**A**BCQSDJ**A**OGC
   I**A**LBBFD**A**BCQSDJ**A**OGC RTO**A**ECFG?UJ**A**IL**A**B**A**B

3. **(C) is correct.** Sixteen C's appear in the box.

   I?BMBTIOPRDFQSDRAB**C**QSDJAOGQJILOPBMJ?
   F?YTRED**C**MJALAUB?GYFGTED**C**FBMAIUWQASX**C**
   GJQJILOPBMJ?F?UJA?TRFDEDSQYTRED**C**MJALA
   UBTIOPRDFQSDRBJIQBJUOLPRTOAE**C**FG?UJAIL
   PQTGJIALBBFDAB**C**QSDJAOG**C**BPLTG?UJAI?BMB
   TIOPRDFQSDRAB**C**QSDJAOG**C**BDRBJIQBJUOLPR
   TOAE**C**FG?UJAILPQTGJIALBBFDAB**C**QSDJAOG**C**
   IALBBFDAB**C**QSDJAOG**C**RTOAE**C**FG?UJAILABAB

4. **(D) is correct.** Eighteen exclamation points (!) appear in the box.

   IOBMBTIOPR**!**FQS**!**RXBXQS**!**ZXOGQZILOPBMZOF
   OYTRE**!**XMZXLXUBOGYFGTE**!**XFBMXIUWQXSXXG
   ZQZRBZIQBZUOLPRTOXEX7GOUZXILPQTGZIXL
   BBF**!**XBXQS**!**ZXOGXIXLBBF**!**XBXQS**!**ZXOGXRTOX
   EXFGOUZXILXBXBILOPBMZOFOUZXOTRF**!**E**!**SQY
   TRE**!**XMZXLXUBTIOPR**!**FQS**!**RBZIQBZXOLPRTOX
   EXFGOUZXILPQTGZIXLBBFTXBXQSTZXOGXBPL
   TGOUZXIOBMBTIOPR**!**FQS**!**RXBXQS**!**XBTG**!** XXXX

5. **(C) is correct.** Fifty X's appear in the box.

   IOBMBTIOPR!FQS!R**X**B**X**QS!Z**X**OGQZILOPBMZOF
   OYTRE!**X**MZ**X**L**X**UBOGYFGTE!**X**FBM**X**IUWQ**X**S**XX**G
   ZQZRBZIQBZUOLPRTO**X**E**X**7GOUZ**X**ILPQTGZI**X**L
   BBF!**X**B**X**QS!Z**X**OG**X**I**X**LBBF!**X**B**X**QS!Z**X**OG**X**RTO**X**
   E**X**FGOUZ**X**IL**X**B**X**BILOPBMZOFOUZ**X**OTRF!E!SQY
   TRE!**X**MZ**X**L**X**UBTIOPR!FQS!RBZIQBZ**X**OLPRTO**X**
   E**X**FGOUZ**X**ILPQTGZI**X**LBBFT**X**B**X**QSTZ**X**OG**X**BPL
   TGOUZ**X**IOBMBTIOPR!FQS!R**X**B**X**QS!**X**BTG! **XXXX**

6. **(B) is correct.** One 7 appears in the box.

   IOBMBTIOPR!FQS!RXBXQS!ZXOGQZILOPBMZOF
   OYTRE!XMZXLXUBOGYFGTE!XFBMXIUWQXSXXG
   ZQZRBZIQBZUOLPRTOXEX**7**GOUZXILPQTGZIXL
   BBF!XBXQS!ZXOGXIXLBBF!XBXQS!ZXOGXRTOX
   EXFGOUZXILXBXBILOPBMZOFOUZXOTRF!E!SQY
   TRE!XMZXLXUBTIOPR!FQS!RBZIQBZXOLPRTOX
   EXFGOUZXILPQTGZIXLBBFTXBXQSTZXOGXBPL
   TGOUZXIOBMBTIOPR!FQS!RXBXQS!XBTG! XXXX

7. **(C) is correct.** Ten S's appear in the box.

```
I4BMBTI4PR!FQS!R7B7QS!0742Q0IL4PBM04F4
YTRE!7M07L7UB42YF2TE!7FBM7IUWQ7S7720Q
0RB0IQB0U4LPRT47E7F24U07ILPQT20I7L04F
4U074TRF!E!SQYTRE!7M07L7UBTI4PR!FQS!RB
0IQB074LPRT47E7F24U07ILPQT20I7LBBFT7B7
QST07427BPLT24U0714BMBTI4PR!FQS!R7B7Q
S!7BT2!77777BBF!7B7QS!0742717LBBF!7B7Q
S!07427 RT47E7F24U07IL7B7BIL4PBMF40B77
```

8. **(B) is correct.** Twenty-three zeros (0) appear in the box.

```
I4BMBTI4PR!FQS!R7B7QS!0742Q0IL4PBM04F4
YTRE!7M07L7UB42YF2TE!7FBM7IUWQ7S7720Q
0RB0IQB0U4LPRT47E7F24U07ILPQT20I7L04F
4U074TRF!E!SQYTRE!7M07L7UBTI4PR!FQS!RB
0IQB074LPRT47E7F24U07ILPQT20I7LBBFT7B7
QST07427BPLT24U0714BMBTI4PR!FQS!R7B7Q
S!7BT2!77777BBF!7B7QS!0742717LBBF!7B7Q
S!07427 RT47E7F24U07IL7B7BIL4PBMF40B77
```

9. **(D) is correct.** Seven M's appear in the box.

```
I4BMBTI4PR!FQS!R7B7QS!0742Q0IL4PBM04F4
YTRE!7M07L7UB42YF2TE!7FBM7IUWQ7S7720
Q0RB0IQB0U4LPRT47E7F24U07ILPQT20I7L04
F4U074TRF!E!SQYTRE!7M07L7UBTI4PR!FQS!RB
0IQB074LPRT47E7F24U07ILPQT20I7LBBFT7B7
QST07427BPLT24U0714BMBTI4PR!FQS!R7B7Q
S!7BT2!77777BBF!7B7QS!0742717LBBF!7B7Q
S!07427 RT47E7F24U07IL7B7BIL4PBMF40B77
```

10. **(B) is correct.** Thirteen L's appear in the box.

```
4LPZT4/E/F24U0/ILPQT20I/L??FT/?/QST0/42/
?PLT24U0/I4?M?TI4PZ!FQS!Z/?/QS!/?T2!/////
??F!/?/QS!0/42/ I/L??F!/?/QS!0/42/ ZT4/E/F24
U0/IL/?/?IL4P?MF40?//I4?M?TI4PZ!FQS!Z/?/Q
S!0/42Q0IL4P?M04F4YTZE!/M0/L/U?42YF2TE!
/F?M/IUWQ/S//20Q0Z?0IQ?0U4LPZT4/E/F24U
0/ILPQT20I/L04F4U0/4TZF!E!SQYTZE!/M0/L/U
?TI4PZ!FQS!Z?TZF!E!SQYTZE!/0IQ?0S
```

11. **(D) is correct.** Fifteen Z's appear in the box.

```
4LPZT4/E/F24U0/ILPQT20I/L??FT/?/QST0/42/
?PLT24U0/I4?M?TI4PZ!FQS!Z/?/QS!/?T2!/////
??F!/?/QS!0/42/ I/L??F!/?/QS!0/42/ ZT4/E/F24
U0/IL/?/?IL4P?MF40?//I4?M?TI4PZ!FQS!Z/?/Q
S!0/42Q0IL4P?M04F4YTZE!/M0/L/U?42YF2TE!
/F?M/IUWQ/S//20Q0Z?0IQ?0U4LPZT4/E/F24U
0/ILPQT20I/L04F4U0/4TZF!E!SQYTZE!/M0/L/U
?TI4PZ!FQS!Z?TZF!E!SQYTZE!/0IQ?0S
```

12. **(A) is correct.** Twelve S's appear in the box.

```
4LPZT4/E/F24U0/ILPQT20I/L??FT/?/QST0/42/
?PLT24U0/I4?M?TI4PZ!FQS!Z/?/QS!/?T2!/////
??F!/?/QS!0/42/I/L??F!/?/QS!0/42/ZT4/E/F24
U0/IL/?/?IL4P?MF40?//I4?M?TI4PZ!FQS!Z/?/Q
S!0/42Q0IL4P?M04F4YTZE!/M0/L/U?42YF2TE!
/F?M/IUWQ/S//20Q0Z?0IQ?0U4LPZT4/E/F24U
0/ILPQT20I/L04F4U0/4TZF!E!SQYTZE!/M0/L/U
?TI4PZ!FQS!Z?TZF!E!SQYTZE!/0IQ?0S
```

13. **(B) is correct.** Eleven plus signs (+) appear in the box.

```
#LPZT#/E*F2#U0/ILPQT20I/L??FT&?/Q+T0/#2
*?PLT2#U0*I#?M?TI#PZ!FQ+!Z/?*Q+!&?T2!***
*&??F!*?*Q+!0*#2&I*L??F!&?/Q+!0/#2* ZT#*E
*F2#U0*IL&?*?IL#P?MF#0?**I#?M?TI#PZ!FQ+!
Z*?*Q+!0*#2Q0IL#P?M0#F#YTZE!&M0*L/U?#2
YF2TE!&F?M&IUWQ&+&/20Q0Z?0IQ?0U#LPZT#
*E/F2#U0*ILPQT20I/L0#F#U0/#TZF!E!+QYTZE
!/M0/L/U?TI#PZ!FQ+!Z?TZF!E!+QYT
```

14. **(D) is correct.** Sixteen slashes (/) appear in the box above.

```
#LPZT#/E*F2#U0/ILPQT20I/L??FT&?/Q+T0/#2*
?PLT2#U0*I#?M?TI#PZ!FQ+!Z/?*Q+!&?T2!****
&??F!*?*Q+!0*#2&I*L??F!&?/Q+!0/#2* ZT#*E*
F2#U0*IL&?*?IL#P?MF#0?**I#?M?TI#PZ!FQ+!Z
*?*Q+!0*#2Q0IL#P?M0#F#YTZE!&M0*L/U?#2Y
F2TE!&F?M&IUWQ&+&/20Q0Z?0IQ?0U#LPZT#*
E/F2#U0*ILPQT20I/L0#F#U0/#TZF!E!+QYTZE!/
M0/L/U?TI#PZ!FQ+!Z?TZF!E!+QYT
```

15. **(B) is correct.** Sixteen F's appear in the box above.

```
#LPZT#/E*F2#U0/ILPQT20I/L??FT&?/Q+T0/#2
*?PLT2#U0*I#?M?TI#PZ!FQ+!Z/?*Q+!&?T2!***
*&??F!*?*Q+!0*#2&I*L??F!&?/Q+!0/#2* ZT#*E
*F2#U0*IL&?*?IL#P?MF#0?**I#?M?TI#PZ!FQ+!
Z*?*Q+!0*#2Q0IL#P?M0#F#YTZE!&M0*L/U?#2
YF2TE!&F?M&IUWQ&+&/20Q0Z?0IQ?0U#LPZT#
*E/F2#U0*ILPQT20I/L0#F#U0/#TZF!E!+QYTZE
!/M0/L/U?TI#PZ!FQ+!Z?TZF!E!+QYT
```

www.ingramcontent.com/pod-product-compliance
Lightning Source LLC
Chambersburg PA
CBHW080746250426
43673CB00062B/1925